D1161879

THE PARTITIONS OF POLAND

THE PARTITIONS OF POLAND

BY

LORD EVERSLEY

HOWARD FERTIG

NEW YORK · 1973

First published in 1915

HOWARD FERTIG, INC. EDITION 1973
Published by arrangement with Ernest Benn Limited

Library of Congress Cataloging in Publication Data

Eversley, George John Shaw-Lefevre, Baron, 1832–1928.
The partitions of Poland.
Reprint of the 1915 ed.

1. Poland—History—Partition period, 1763–1796. I. Title.
DK434.E9 1973 943.8'02 79–80547

PRINTED IN THE UNITED STATES OF AMERICA
BY NOBLE OFFSET PRINTERS, INC.

PREFACE

MANY years ago I made very full notes of the Partitions of Poland, mainly from the accounts, spread over several detached chapters, in their *Histories of the French Revolution*, by von Sybel and Albert Sorel. My then interest in the subject arose chiefly from the close connection between the tragic events in Poland and the fortunes of France in the revolutionary wars of 1792-5, a matter which, it seemed to me, had not been sufficiently appreciated by English historians. Other claims on my time, however, prevented my pursuing further the project of writing on the subject.

But when, at the commencement of the present great war, each of the three Powers who, in 1772 and 1793-5, had been concerned in dismembering Poland, announced its intention, at the conclusion of the war, to do its best to reunite the Polish provinces under some form of autonomous government, it occurred to me that I might, with possible advantage to a discussion of the questions which will arise, expand my notes into a succinct and popular account of the three partitions.

Sybel wrote with a very strong bias in favour of his country. Though he described with perfect fairness most, though not all, of the misdeeds of Prussia, and admitted that her conduct in some of them amounted to "utter perfidy," he ended by defending and justifying them as necessary in the interest of the German State. Sorel wrote from a very different point of view. I have collated the accounts of these two historians, and supplemented them from other sources. It will be seen that I have come to conclusions the very opposite to those of Sybel. I have also ventured to differ from Carlyle, in his *History of Frederick the Great*, as to the responsibility of the Prussian King for the first partition, and as to his commendation of the whole transaction.

I have consulted many other books on Poland, among them Rulhiére's *Histoire de l'Anarchie Polonaise*, Sorel's *Questions d'Orient*, Fletcher's *Poland* (1830), von Moltke's *Poland*, the condemned chapter on "Poland" in the *Cambridge History of Modern Europe*, Skrine's *Russia*, Prince Bülow's *Imperial Germany*, and many memoirs of the time. I have also consulted, at the Record Office, the correspondence between the British Foreign Office and its diplomatic agents during the period dealt with, the importance of which the late Mr. Lecky pointed out when referring to the First Partition of Poland in his *History of England in the Eighteenth Century*.

Of the four maps included in this volume, the first two show the original Kingdom of Poland, before 1772, and the parts taken from it by the three neighbouring Powers in the three partitions. I have found much difficulty in deciding as to the boundaries of the second partition, as the authorities differ very much on the subject. I have been guided in this respect mainly by the map given in the *Cambridge History of Modern Europe*. The authorities differ still more as to the areas and populations of the shares taken by the three Powers. The figures which I give in the text must be taken with some reservation. The third map gives the boundaries of the Grand Duchy of Warsaw, as settled by the Treaty of Tilsit in 1807, and added to, at the expense of Austria, in 1809, and also the limits of the Kingdom of Poland, under the suzerainty of the Tsar of Russia, as prescribed by the Treaty of Vienna, 1815, and added to by the Emperor Alexander of his free will. In the fourth map I have endeavoured to show the present distribution of the Polish population. It is not possible to define the boundaries by distinct lines, as the proportion of Poles to Germans, Russians, and Ruthenians, gradually changes from 80 to 20 per cent. and less. The map shows at a glance the complexity of the questions which will arise when the time comes for re-uniting the dismembered Polish districts into a single autonomous State.

I have to thank Lord Bryce for his valuable suggestions, and Lady Byles for her kind help.

E.

CONTENTS

THE PARTITIONS OF POLAND

CHAPTER I

THE POLISH ANARCHY

A SURVEY of the map of Europe, as it now is, compared with what it was a century and a half ago, shortly before the first partition of Poland, shows many remarkable changes in the constitution of nations, and their relative strength to one another. In the interval referred to, two great nationalities, Germany and Italy, after long deferred hopes, have been consolidated by the union, more or less complete, of several of their parts, previously separated, and by the freeing, in the case of Italy, of other parts from foreign rule. One great Empire, that of Turkey, founded on conquest by a barbaric horde from the East, has been driven from all but a small corner of its dominions in Europe, and Greece, Servia, Montenegro, Roumania, and Bulgaria have thereby achieved independence and have been acknowledged as nations. In one case only during the period, that of Poland, has a nation which formerly, and for many centuries, held a proud position in Europe, entitling it to be ranked as one of the greater Powers, ceased to exist, in the sense that its corporate existence and independence have been destroyed, and that its territory and people have been divided among neighbouring Powers, who have done their best to obliterate the very name of the race, and to fuse them with their own people, by enforcing identity of language, religion, and laws.

This principle of nationality, as the main element of a State, has only been fully recognized in recent times. So late as the first half of the last century identity of race and language was little regarded in the conception of a modern State. The House of Hapsburg, the House of Bourbon, the Hohenzollerns, and the Romanoffs extended their Empires, without any regard to the above considerations. The rounding off of their territories, the possession of strategic points, the access to great navigable rivers, or to the sea, were objects aimed at, without any regard to the nationality, or the wishes of the population affected by the annexations. In this view it is necessary to distinguish between the ethnographical Poland, the country actually inhabited by the distinctive race of Poles, and the historical or geographical Poland.

The historical Poland, in 1770, was a vast country, extending from the Baltic almost to the Black Sea, and lying between Russia and Germany, with an area of about 280,000 square miles, and a population roughly estimated at eleven and a half millions. It stood third in the list of European countries as regards its extent, and fifth as regards its population. But two-thirds at least of this vast area were inhabited, not by Poles but by other races, Slavs and Germans, and the actual number of people of Polish race was probably not more than seven millions.

In the north-east of this country lay the province of Lithuania, vastly exceeding the area of Poland proper, a thinly peopled district, of which not more than one-seventh was cultivated, and the rest consisted of forests and waste lands. It was inhabited by people of another race, with a different language, of very inferior culture, and with more affinity to the Russians, and, like them, drawing their religion from the Greek Church. This province had been originally an independent State, but in 1386 it was united to Poland by the marriage of Jagellon, its Grand

Duke, with the daughter of the last of the Polish native kings. Thenceforth, for little short of two centuries, the Jagellons were Kings of Poland and Grand Dukes of Lithuania. The two States remained distinct till 1560, when Sigismund, the last of the Jagellon line, succeeded, with the full assent of the Lithuanians, in effecting a complete union of the two States, known as the Kingdom of Poland.

There was a central government and a single Diet for the united kingdom thus constituted. But Lithuania preserved in a large measure its local institutions and its language. In the course, however, of the two hundred years which followed, Polish ideals and culture spread in the province, and the Polish language came into general use among the educated classes, and for official purposes.

In the south-east of Poland were the Ukraine and Volhynia, inhabited by another branch of Slavs, the Ruthenians, with a language nearly akin to that of Russia, and also members of the Greek Church. In the north-west there was a considerable district known as West Prussia, of which the larger part was inhabited by Germans. This district, on the shore of the Baltic, separated East Prussia from Brandenburg, and other parts of Germany, which formed the Kingdom of Prussia. Making deduction for these non-Polish territories, there was an ethnographical Poland of about 80,000 square miles, coinciding with what is still inhabited by people speaking the Polish language, namely, the whole of Great Poland, the Prussian province of Posen, about one-half of the province of West Prussia, and one-third of Silesia, the last three belonging to Germany, and about one-half of Galicia, with Cracow as its capital, now under the dominion of Austria. This ethnographical Poland, at the time we refer to, had a population estimated roughly at seven and a half millions, increased at the present time to nearly twenty millions. The Poles of this district form, in the main, a compact and homogeneous people, though the boundaries between them and other peoples, in some directions, are not easy to define. In point of population they are seventh in the list of nationalities in Europe. They are exceeded only by Russia, Germany, Great Britain, France, Italy, and Spain. They greatly exceed any of the smaller nationalities, such as the Swedes, the Norwegians and Danes, the Dutch, the Portuguese, and the others above referred to.

How it came about that to the east of the

centre of Europe there was a Slavonic race, with a language distinct from those of other Slavs, and Roman Catholics in religion, bounded on the east by other Slavs of the Greek Church and on the north-west by Germans of the Lutheran faith, it is foreign to our purpose to discuss. Much literature has been devoted to the subject, without very definite conclusion. It is sufficient for us that they are there. "J'y suis j'y reste" may be said of the Polish race. It is very certain that they are a brave and gifted people, capable of high culture. In the fifteenth century they formed one of the most civilized nations in Europe. They reached their apogee when their warrior king Sobieski, in 1683, saved Europe from being overwhelmed by an Ottoman invasion, by marching to Vienna with an army of 30,000 men, and defeating, in combination with the Austrians, a Turkish army of 200,000 men, a most signal service to Western civilization. Thenceforward, there was distinct and continuous decadence, till the Kingdom of Poland was extinguished in 1795.

The causes of this decadence and ultimate ruin have been recognized and fully admitted by every historian who has written of Poland, and the result was long predicted by its rulers and others. The country was afflicted with the most vicious Constitution which has ever been devised by man. Its main defects were not of very ancient standing. The first of them was that the monarchy of Poland was elective, and not hereditary. Till the failure of the Jagellon line of kings, in the eighteenth century, the Constitution of Poland was practically, though not theoretically, an hereditary monarchy, very much like those of other contemporary States in Europe. But on the death, in 1672, of Sigismund, leaving no heir, the monarchy became actually elective, and thenceforth, on the demise of a Polish king, his successor was elected by the Diet, and no hereditary claim was admitted. At a time when in most other States in Europe the monarchical principle was strengthened and centralized, and wider powers were conferred on the King, as representing the whole people, giving consistency and stability to the State, and better protection to the labouring classes against the local tyranny of feudal lords, in Poland the reverse took place. The landowners there, who constituted an exclusive caste of nobles, succeeded in strengthening and magnifying their influence in the State, and instead of raising the status of the King, and increasing his powers, were continually engaged in limiting and circumscribing them, till they were reduced almost to a nullity.

The elections to the throne often resulted in the choice of foreign princelings, who were placed at the head of affairs in Poland, without previous knowledge of the country, and without any sense of permanency of the throne in their families. This led to violent competitions and contests. Neighbouring States were greatly concerned in them. It was of great importance to obtain the influence and support of Poland in their rivalries with one another. Factions were therefore formed and subsidized in Poland by the most powerful of its neighbours, and when a vacancy to the throne occurred the country was thrown into a turmoil by these rival interests. Bribery was largely resorted to, and force, or threats of force, were used to secure the election of a candidate favoured by some neighbouring Power. Not unfrequently a foreign army marched into the country in support of some candidate. The nobles took the opportunity of the election of a King to enter into a new contract with him, putting further restraint on his powers. These arrangements were called *pacta conventa*.

The King had no real power. He was nominally the head of the Executive and of the army. The Executive consisted of the chief officers of state, over whom the King had no real control, for he could not dismiss them. They were appointed for life. The army, small in number, was often left without pay. In time of war the provincial palatines were bound to summon to arms the nobles of their districts, but there were no means of enforcing this duty.

The class of so-called nobles consisted, not merely of the existing feudal owners of the land, but of the descendants, however remote, of past members of it—a very numerous body more or less dependent on a few territorial magnates. If any member of this class engaged in trade he lost his claims in it. Fusion, therefore, into other classes of the community was practically prevented. The adult males of this body, numbering, it was estimated, 160,000, supplied the fighting force of the country in time of war. They alone elected the members of the Polish Diet. Other classes, including the burghers of the towns, were excluded from representation. Though there was nominal equality in this class of nobles, the feudal magnates, through their dependents, exercised overwhelming influence in the Diet. It resulted that the Constitution of Poland was that of an aristocratic republic.

The King being a mere figurehead, it might be expected that the nobles, acting through the Diet, would constitute a strong executive and legislative power, and would govern the country. But this was very far from being the case. By a most strange and exceptional provision of the Constitution, the power for good or evil of the Diet was neutralized and almost extinguished. There seems to have been from early times a passion for equality among the class of persons who had the status of nobles. The decisions of the Diet were only valid if agreed to unanimously, and a single member could prevent legislation by opposing his veto to it by the simple words "*Nie pozwalam*" ("I do not consent"). This was called the *Liberum Veto*. It practically paralysed the assembly, and prevented executive or legislative action on their part. It was, however, possible in grave crises, when the country required immediate legislation, for the Diet, with the general assent of its members, to suspend the Liberum Veto, and to confederate itself, as it was termed. In such a case, a simple majority of the Diet had power to legislate. It was, however, on very rare occasions that such an expedient could be resorted to. The majority of the Diet at times compelled agreement of a small minority by physical force. It will be seen that in recent years, when Russia obtained a commanding influence in Poland, it overcame the constitutional difficulty of the Liberum Veto by deporting the members of a factious minority to Siberia. But in the period before the Russian intervention the Liberum Veto was a complete paralysis to the executive and legislative power of the Diet. It was a representation of minorities carried to an extreme.

Another cause of anarchy was the custom which had grown up of any number of nobles, dissatisfied, with the action or inaction of the Diet, to summon a rival Confederation, and even to support it by an appeal to arms. There appears to have been no force in the central government sufficient to prevent such gatherings. Under the operation of these great and glaring defects of the Constitution, the Polish nation went headlong to ruin. Legislation became impossible. The most necessary reforms were indefinitely postponed. The nobility were unrestrained in their cruel local tyrannies. The condition of the cultivators of the soil became more servile and degraded than ever. There was no cohesion in the State. Poland was at the mercy of its neighbours. Whichever of them chose to send its army into Poland, for any purpose, could do so without fear of opposition. This did not mean that the country welcomed the invader, or that there was disaffection to its central government, or rather lack of government, which would cause disruption. On the contrary, the great province of Lithuania, in spite of its affinities to Russia, was as much averse to being incorporated in that Empire, as was the purely Polish province; and the German districts of East Poland showed no desire to be annexed by Prussia. The purely German city of Danzig made vigorous resistance to the Prussian invaders in 1793.

These defects, and the evil results of the Constitution, were fully admitted by all patriotic Poles, and were exposed by successive Kings of Poland in public utterances. Many were the predictions and warnings that if a remedy were not applied, ruin would come to the State, and Poland would be partitioned by its greedy and menacing neighbours. One of the most interesting of these was a speech delivered to the Diet by Casimir, King of Poland, in 1667, on the occasion of his resigning the throne and retiring into private life.

"Magnanimous Polish gentlemen," he said, "you are a glorious republic, and have *Nie pozwalam* and strange methods of business and of behaviour to your Kings and others. We have often fought together, been beaten together by our enemies and by ourselves; and at last I, for my share, have had enough of it. I intend for Paris, religious literary pursuits, and the society of Ninon de l'Enclos. I wished to say before going, that according to all record, ancient and modern, of the way of God Almighty to the world, there was not heretofore, nor do I expect there can henceforth be, a human society that would stick together on those terms. Believe me, ye Polish Chevaliers, without superior, except in heaven, if your glorious republic continue to be managed in such manner, not good will come of it, but evil. The day will arrive, and the day perhaps is not far off, when this glorious republic will get torn into shreds hither thither; be stuffed into the pockets of covetous neighbours, Brandenburg, Muscovy, Austria, and find itself reduced to zero, and abolished from the face of the world. I speak these words from the fullness of my heart and on behest of friendship and conviction alone, having the honour at this moment to bid you and your republic a very long farewell. Good morning for the last time." *

Another warning of the same kind, also uttered by one of its Kings, Stanislaus Leszczynski,

* Carlyle, vi. 405.

in 1734, in the hope of rousing the Poles to a sense of their danger, was as follows:—

"I reflect with dread upon the perils which surround us. What forces have we to resist our neighbours? Do we trust to the faith of treaties? How many samples have we of the frequent neglect of even the most solemn agreements! We imagine that our neighbours are interested in our preservation by their mutual jealousies, a vain prejudice which deceives us, a ridiculous infatuation, which formerly lost the Hungarians their liberty, and will surely deprive us of ours if, depending on such a frivolous hope, we continue unarmed. Our turn will come, no doubt; either we shall be the prey of some famous conqueror, or perhaps even the neighbouring Powers will combine to divide our States." *

It is very certain that a remedy would have been found for this intolerable anarchy, and would have been carried into effect by the Diet itself, as, in fact, was attempted, a few years later, by an overwhelming majority of it, if it had not been that Poland was surrounded by implacable and relentless enemies, who were bent on dismembering their neighbour. These Powers were fully aware that the anarchy in Poland afforded the certain prospect to them of carrying into effect their evil intents, and they were determined to prevent any reforms

* Fletcher's *Poland*, p. 261.

which could remove the defects and strengthen the Polish State.

It was the bad fortune also of Poland, at the time, when its leading men became fully conscious of the defects of its Constitution, and were preparing to apply remedies, that the thrones of two of its three neighbouring States were filled by sovereigns of overweening ambition and of exceptional vigour. Catherine II, Empress of Russia, who was mainly responsible during her long reign for the three partitions of Poland, was one of the most remarkable women in history. The daughter of a minor Prince of the German Empire, she was married at a very early age to the Grand Duke Peter, the heir to the Russian throne, a brutal drunkard, who neglected her, and who not only tolerated but encouraged her infidelities to him, and insultingly disclaimed in public, in her presence, that he was the father of her son. Her appearance, at this time of her life, has been described by that enigmatical personage the Chevalier D'Éon, who was in the pay of France, as a spy, at the Russian Court. "The Grand Duchess," he wrote three years before she became Empress, "is romantic, ardent, passionate; her eyes are brilliant, their look fascinating, glassy, like those of a wild beast. Her brow is high, and, if I mistake not, an awful future is written on that brow. She is kind and affable; but when she comes near me I draw back with a movement I cannot control. She frightens me."

Within a short time, after the accession of Peter as Tsar, Catherine was privy to his dethronement, and subsequent murder by conspirators, of whom Alexis Orloff, brother of Gregory Orloff, her handsome paramour, was leader. She then, by the same agencies, supplanted her son, the Grand Duke Paul, who had no real claim to succeed his putative father, and became possessed of supreme power in the State. In one aspect of her life she was a woman of the lowest type. She sounded the depths of sensuality and shameless immorality. She is said to have spent twenty millions sterling of the public money on a succession of favourites, most of them men of most worthless character. But though she gave her person, she never surrendered her will to any man. In the other department of her life she showed most eminent qualities. She achieved absolute power such as no other sovereign of her time, or few of all time, possessed. In many respects her Government was enlightened, tolerant, and beneficial to her subjects. But at the same time she was cruel and pitiless if any one crossed her will. She had a powerful intellect. She was lively and witty in her conversation. She corresponded on equal terms with the ablest philosophers of her time, with Voltaire, Diderot, D'Alembert, and Grimm.

She was an excellent judge of men, and selected her agents, and maintained or dismissed them with unfailing courage and success. She was consumed with ambition for the territorial expansion of her adopted country. She was capable of devising schemes for this purpose, which required long years for their development, and unremitting application in giving effect to them. She said of herself on one occasion to the French Ambassador: "Europe has its eyes fixed on me. I think, in fact, that Russia deserves attention. No judgment can be formed of me for some years, and meanwhile I play the part of a coquette to all the other sovereigns of Europe." *

She allowed no considerations of public morality or faith of treaties to interfere with

* Sorel, *Questions d'Orient*, p. 12.

her schemes. But she never lost control of them, or of herself, and it was remarkable how much restraint she exhibited in her policy, and with how little real expenditure of force she accomplished her schemes. "I came," she said, "to Russia a poor girl. Russia has dowered me richly, but I have paid her back with Azof, the Crimea, and Poland."

It is certain that from a very early period of her reign this bold, proud, and self-reliant woman determined to extend her territory at the expense of Poland. It will be seen that it was claimed on her behalf that thirty years of her life were devoted to this object with relentless determination.

Her principal instigator and abettor in the first partition was Frederick the Great of Prussia, on whose pre-eminent qualities as a general, and as an administrator of his country in times of peace, it is unnecessary for us to dilate. It will be well, however, to refer briefly to the principles which actuated him in his international relations.

Frederick, in his younger days, just before his accession to the throne of Prussia, wrote an able refutation of Machiavelli's well-known work on "The Prince." The Florentine casuist, we need hardly say, maintained in this that a sovereign is not bound, in public affairs, by the moral code, which is regarded as incumbent on individuals, and that he might go to any lengths of bad faith and deception, provided he had in view only the interests of his country. Frederick repelled these principles with horror and indignation. He insisted, in forcible language, that a sovereign is bound to observe the same code of morality as other men in private life, and that integrity and good faith must be his sole rule of conduct in public affairs. His book, entitled "The Anti-Machiavelli," was enthusiastically applauded by his friend, the sage philosopher Voltaire, who undertook the publication of it, at The Hague, in 1740.

In the same year, Frederick succeeded to the throne of Prussia. He very soon flung aside the great principles which he had so strongly insisted upon in his book. Beyond any of his contemporary monarchs he was conspicuous for following the precepts laid down in "The Prince." Territorial aggrandizement was to him, as to Catherine, the main object of his foreign policy. He pursued it without regard to morality or good faith. He was foremost of the Hohenzollerns in propounding as a policy for himself and his successors that "might makes right," and that no treaty need stand in the way when the interest of the State points in an opposite direction.

"There is no alliance," he wrote, "or agreement in the world that can be regarded as effective if it is not fastened by the band of common and reciprocal interests."

"If a ruler is obliged to sacrifice his own person for the welfare of his subjects, he is all the more obliged to sacrifice treaty engagements, the continuance of which would be harmful to his country. Is it better that a nation should perish or that a sovereign should break his treaty?"

"I give you a problem to solve," he said to his councillors on one occasion. "When you have the advantage are you to use it or not?"

It was this complete absence of morality and this cynical disregard of treaties and alliances, which signalized the two great territorial acquisitions of Prussia in Frederick's reign—namely, Silesia and Poland. It will be seen that his successor, Frederick William II, pursued the same policy in the second and third partitions of Poland, with exhibitions of perfidy and meanness, which the great Frederick would perhaps have been ashamed of.

The third coadjutor, Austria, was in a somewhat different position. Ever since the assistance rendered by the Poles, under Sobieski, in the defeat of the Turks, and the saving of Vienna, it had been the policy of Austrian statesmen to support Poland as a useful buffer State, and a possible ally against either Russia or Turkey. Hatred and jealousy of the growing power of Prussia confirmed them in this policy. But Austria alone was not able to withstand a combination of Russia and Prussia, especially when it was engaged in war with France. The position, therefore, of its rulers as regards Poland was generally this: "We have no wish for its dismemberment, but if it must take place, we will insist on having a share in the plunder." On this plea of her advisers, the Empress Maria Theresa, the contemporary of Catherine, who prided herself on her virtues, and her regard for public morality, and the faith of treaties, was persuaded, much against her will, to join in the combination against Poland, or, at all events, to claim indemnity out of its dismembered territory. Her grandson, Francis, who was Emperor during the second and third partitions, went much further to meet his two rival conspirators, and did not lag behind them in avidity for territorial aggrandizement, or in want of scruple in achieving it.

Against such a remarkable combination of intellect, determination, perfidy, and lawlessness the unfortunate Poles, with their anarchic Constitution, their lack of a strong Executive, and their paralysed Diet, were quite unable to make resistance.

CHAPTER II

THE FIRST PARTITION (1772)

In 1763, the throne of Poland was vacant, by the death of Augustus III, Elector of Saxony, and in the following year a Diet was summoned at Warsaw to elect a successor. With a view to this a treaty was made between the Empress Catherine and Frederick the Great of Prussia. They agreed to propose for the throne of Poland, and support with all their power, a native of that country, Count Stanislaus Poniatowski, a young man not of high birth, on his father's side, but through his mother, nephew of Prince Czartoryski, the wealthiest and most powerful of the nobles in Lithuania, of which he was also Chancellor. This Poniatowski had nothing to recommend him for this position but his exceeding good looks, and his pleasant and engaging manners, which had won him a favourable reception in the *salons* of Paris and London. He was otherwise wholly wanting in the qualifications necessary for kingship, at a time so full of peril, as the sequel will show, for Poland. His good looks had already brought him *bonnes fortunes*, for in 1756 he had been attached to the suite of Hanbury Williams, the British Ambassador at St. Petersburg, and had there attracted, as Williams expected and intended, the attention, and a good deal more, of the young Grand Duchess, the wife of the heir to the throne, soon to become the Empress Catherine. Poniatowski was the second of the very long list of paramours of this dissolute woman, and occupied this position with the full assent of her husband, the Grand Duke Peter.

When Williams was recalled, Poniatowski was appointed Minister of Poland at the Russian Court, doubtless because of his intimacy and supposed interest with the Grand Duchess. Later, owing to a political intrigue, he was sent about his business to Poland. But Catherine, after she had become Empress of Russia, bore her *ci-devant* lover in mind, and when the vacancy occurred in the throne of Poland, determined to foist him upon its people as their King. She was so shrewd a judge of men, and so successful in the choice of agents for carrying out her policy, that we may be very certain that she had taken accurate measure of the mean capacities of Poniatowski, and had foreseen that he would be a compliant tool in her interest, ready to obey her behests. At all events, she felt that he would give no strength to his country, and would be unable to resist her schemes, whatever they might be, for its undoing. To his urgent messages for support to his candidature she sent the laconic reply: "I send Keyserling [her Ambassador] to Poland with orders to make you or your cousin, Adam Czartoryski, King." * It was as though she were casting her shoe over this decadent State. It was enough to secure the election of her protégé. She also intimated that if there was opposition to the election of Poniatowski, he would be supported by Russian and Prussian troops.

In the treaty concerning the candidature of this featherhead, the two Powers—Russia and Prussia—had also, with Machiavellian intent, agreed to maintain the Polish Constitution, in all its glaring defects, and especially to resist the abolition of the Liberum Veto, and the proposal to make the throne hereditary in the

* Fletcher's *Poland*, p. 197.

future, which the treaty described as injurious and dangerous to neighbouring States.

There was a strong party of Polish nobles opposed to the election of Poniatowski, and in favour of the Elector of Saxony, son of the late King. But the Czartoryskis and the many great nobles, in alliance with that family, did their best to support him. Prince Czartoryski was strongly in favour of reform of the Constitution, and hoped by electing the nominee of the Empress to obtain her consent to the measures, which he knew to be necessary for the salvation of the State. It will be seen that he was completely outwitted by Catherine, and that the election proved to be fatal to his reforms, and to the very existence of Poland.

The election of Poniatowski by the Diet was only effected by the most profuse bribery. For this purpose Catherine depleted the Russian Treasury, and even neglected to pay her troops. Great sums were also expended on behalf of the Saxon candidate. Money was poured into Warsaw, justifying the old taunt that Poland lived on the sale of its throne. But money alone was not sufficient on this occasion. The Empress supported her candidate by an army of 15,000 men, who appeared at Warsaw, and surrounded the Diet on the day of election; while a much larger force was stationed on the frontier, ready to invade Poland, if necessary. By dint of these threats of force, and of profuse bribery, Poniatowski was elected King on September 7, 1764, and reigned under the name of Stanislaus.

But though Stanislaus was elected King, the real authority remained with the Russian agent, Prince Repnin, who made no secret of his intention to have his way. "You see," he said to Stanislaus, "I am your master. You can only retain your Crown by submission to me." * Stanislaus was mortally afraid of his patron, and though he had occasionally some *soupçon* of patriotism, he gave way whenever Repnin insisted. Repnin also dominated the Diet by the undisguised use of force, and by deporting to Siberia any deputies who refused to vote as he desired.

A pretext for further intervention by Russia and Prussia was soon found in the question of religious intolerance, which had become a serious one in Poland. The country had for centuries been remarkably free from religious

* Fletcher's *Poland*, p. 221.

strife. Its Constitution, while recognizing Roman Catholicism as the national established Church, prescribed toleration for all other religious sects. It had afforded asylum to Jews in great numbers, when they were driven by persecution from Germany and Russia. The religious wars between Catholics and Lutherans, of the sixteenth century, had not extended to Poland. The immense majority of people in Great Poland were Roman Catholics. Those in Lithuania were mostly members of the Greek Church ; while in the provinces bordering on the Baltic there were great numbers of Lutherans. These had all been treated on terms of equality. Of late years, however, the Jesuits had gained a footing in Great Poland, and had succeeded in inciting the people to measures of intolerance.

In 1756, the Polish Diet adopted a law excluding all but members of the established Roman Catholic Church from holding offices under the State, and in other ways interfering with unorthodox religions. This action of the Diet was the cause of discontent on the part of Dissidents, as they were called. Russia took up the cause of members of the Greek Church and Prussia that of the Lutherans. By the treaty of 1764, they undertook to re-establish the Dissidents in their privileges. In 1767, the Diet, at the dictation of the Russian Ambassador, and after deporting to Siberia some over-zealous Roman Catholic bishops, voted the repeal of the laws directed against the Dissidents.

In 1768, the Polish Diet gave its sanction to a treaty with Russia, by which that Power guaranteed the integrity of Poland as a consideration for the undertaking of the Poles to maintain inviolable and unaltered their anarchical Constitution. This involved the complete subjection of the State to Russia. The minority of members of the Diet, when defeated on these two questions, and compelled to yield to the threats of Russia, confederated at Bar, and agitated there for a restoration of the supremacy of the Roman Catholic religion as the Established Church in Poland, and the exclusion of all Dissidents from public employment, and also for a repudiation of the treaty with Russia. They took up arms to enforce these demands. They applied for help to the Turks, who thereupon declared war with Russia. These proceedings afforded an excuse to Russia for sending more troops into Poland in support of the Diet of Warsaw. Prussia also followed the example of Russia, and sent troops across the frontier and occupied the Palatinate of Wormie. Austria, who favoured the confederates of Bar, rather than the Diet of Warsaw, followed suit, and sent its soldiers into the parts of Poland adjacent to its own. It further revived an ancient claim of the Crown of Hungary to the small Palatinate of Zips, adjoining that kingdom, and without waiting the issue of negotiations, forcibly occupied it by troops.

An outbreak of plague in Poland in 1770 afforded a further excuse for their action by the three neighbouring Powers. It was thought necessary to employ troops to enforce *cordons sanitaires*, so as to prevent the extension of the plague to their own adjoining territories. A wide discretion was exercised, and the cordons were gradually advanced into Poland, so as to include much territory, to which the Powers might later make claim of acquisition. It was evident, therefore, that the vultures were gathering round Poland expectant of prey.

The entry of so many foreign troops into Poland led, not unnaturally, to the general belief that a dismemberment of the unfortunate kingdom was in contemplation by the neighbouring Powers. For many years past the partition of Poland had been in the air. A scheme with this object had been first proposed by a King of Poland. In 1733, Augustus II, hoping to make the throne of Poland hereditary in his House of Saxony, came to the conclusion that the only way of appeasing the jealousy of the neighbouring Courts would be to agree with them for a cession of part of his kingdom, and he made overtures to this effect to Frederick William I, the King of Prussia. Frederick the Great, then Prince Royal, urged his father to avail himself of this opportunity of adding Prussian Poland to his dominions.* The death of Augustus, however, put an end to the scheme. But Frederick kept always in mind a territorial aggrandizement in this direction. For a time, however, he dissembled his views, and when challenged on the subject by the Ambassador of Austria, at the time of his treaty with Russia in 1764, he said:—

"I am sure that your Court is alarmed about the treaty, and that at Vienna it is believed that we have already decided on the partition of Poland. But you will see that the contrary is the case."

* Sorel, *Questions d'Orient*, p. 19.

The Empress Catherine also thought it well to deny rumours to the same effect. In a circular to her diplomatic agents she wrote: "We have never had the intention, nor have we the need, to extend the limits of our Empire, which already consist of a large part of the terrestrial globe."

These disclaimers were to be taken *cum grano salis*. The rumours were only somewhat premature. In November 1768 Frederick wrote his political testament, in which he defined the task of his successor. In the course of it he declared Prussian Poland to be the main object to be aimed at. "It seems," he said, "that the great obstacle will come from Russia. It will be better perhaps to gain this province, bit by bit, by negotiation, rather than by conquest. In the case when Russia may need our assistance it will be possible to obtain what we want." It would seem that very shortly after writing this, he must have come to the conclusion that the condition of Poland, and the fact that all three Powers were sending troops into it, afforded an opportunity, and that it would be better to effect partition at once by negotiation and intrigue, rather than leave the job to his successor. In a letter to his brother, Prince Henry, early in 1769, he wrote:—

"Two courses are open to us: either to arrest Russia in its course of immense conquests, or, what will be the wisest course, to endeavour by good management to draw advantage from it. What," he added, "could Austria do? She would be compelled to remain faithful to her French alliance. In such case she would be compelled to take the part of the Turks and Poles, or she would be seduced by Russia, who would offer to her a part of the cake, and Prussia in such case would find itself between Austria and Russia. To find a way out of this dilemma it will be necessary to indemnify Russia for the costs of her war with Turkey, to separate Austria from France, and to satisfy the Court of Vienna in such a way as to remove the temptation to it of an alliance with Russia." *

The letter shows that Frederick had then in contemplation a tripartite arrangement with the Courts of Russia and Austria for dividing Poland. In this view, on February 2, 1769, he made the first step towards a scheme of this kind by writing to Baron Solms, his Ambassador at St. Petersburg, and directing him to suggest to the Russian Government that it should offer to the Court of Vienna, in return for assistance in war against the Turks, certain provinces of Poland, and that Prussia should have Prussian Poland and the province of Wormie and the

* Sorel, *Questions d'Orient*, p. 42.

right of suzerainty over Danzig, and that Russia also should take compensation in part of Poland.*

A few days later, on February 16th, he wrote again to Solms, explaining his views as to Austria: "If Austria gets no part of Poland, all the hatred of the Poles will be turned against us. They would thus regard the Austrians as their protectors, and the latter would gain so much of prestige and influence with them, that they would have thousands of opportunities for intrigue of all kinds in that country."

These letters indicate clearly the scheme of partition which was actually carried into effect three years later. Solms long hesitated whether to act on this suggestion of Frederick or not. He thought that Russia would prefer to make Poland a completely subject dependency, rather than divide it with her neighbours. He decided, however, to make the effort, and he broached the subject with Count Panine, the Russian Minister of Foreign Affairs, who was always in the pay of Frederick. He found, as he expected, that Minister distinctly averse to the scheme of dismemberment of Poland. He

* Sorel, p. 69.

favoured the alternative of gradually reducing it, unaltered as to its boundaries, to an abject dependency on Russia, but without actually incorporating it as a Russian province. It appears, however, that the proposal was submitted by Panine to the Empress, and that she was more favourable to a scheme of partition than her Minister. She was afraid that war with Austria and Turkey combined might risk her favoured position in Poland. Frederick, by working on these fears, and at the same time stimulating her ambitions, gradually won her completely to his scheme. There was, however, long delay. Frederick, in his Memoirs, explains the causes of this :—

"The slowness and irresolution of the Russians protracted the conclusion of the treaty of partition; the negotiations hung chiefly on the possession of the city of Danzig. The Russians pretended that they had guaranteed the liberty of this little republic; but it was, in fact, the English who, jealous of the Prussians, protected the liberty of this maritime town, and who prompted the Empress of Russia not to consent to the demands of the Prussian majesty. It was requisite, however, for the King to determine; and as it was evident that the mastery of the Vistula would in time subject that city, he decided that it was not necessary to stop such an important negotiation for an advantage *which, in fact, was only deferred;* therefore his Majesty relaxed the demand. . . . After so many obstacles had been removed the secret contract was signed at

Petersburg on February 17, 1772. . . . The month of June was fixed on for taking possession, and it was agreed that the Empress-Queen should be invited to join the two contracting parties and join in the partition."

Meanwhile Frederick was also negotiating and intriguing at Vienna. He had even more difficulty here, in the first istance, than at St. Petersburg. Direct negotiation between the two Courts of Russia and Austria was impossible. The two Empresses hated one another. The Austrian spoke of Catherine contemptuously as "that woman." Frederick acted as the honest broker between the two.

It has been shown that the traditional policy of Austria was to maintain the integrity of the Polish kingdom. This policy had been steadily pursued by Prince Kaunitz, during the long time he had been Chief Minister in Vienna. Kaunitz has been described by Frederick as "a solemn, arrogant, mouthing, brow-beating kind of man, with a clear intellect twisted by perversities of temper, especially by a self-conceit and arrogance which are boundless. He did not talk, but preached. At the smallest interruption he would stop short in indignant surprise." * He must, all the same, have been a man of great

* Carlyle, vi. p. 464.

force of character, and with the power of imposing his policy on the rulers of Austria, for he held his post for over forty years. During this time he showed himself a subtle politician, without scruples of any kind. He had no small opinion of himself. "Heaven," he said, "is a hundred years in forming a great mind for the restoration of an Empire, and it then rests another hundred years; in this event I tremble for the fate which awaits this monarchy."

Maria Theresa, when the question of joining in a partition scheme was first mooted to her, was very averse to it. She was much ageing. She was devoting herself to religion, while nursing her grief for her late husband. She had qualms of conscience. She had some sense of right and wrong. Possibly she was influenced by her spiritual advisers, for Rome was much interested in Catholic Poland. Kaunitz, also, in the first instance, was opposed to it. The Empress wrote to him, in what she described as "a Jeremiad":—

"I do not understand the political system which permits, in the case where two Powers make use of their superiority to oppress an innocent opponent, a third, by way of precaution for the future and convenience for the present, to imitate and follow their example. A prince has no other rights than a private person. The greatness and the maintenance of his state will not enter into the matter when he shall have to render account of what he has done. What will France, Spain, and England say of the transaction? Let us pass for feeble rather than for dishonest folk. Let us endeavour to reduce the pretensions of these others rather than join them in a partition so unequal." *

She also wrote to her son that her maxim in political affairs, which she owed to Kaunitz, was "honesty and candour and no duplicity." By her direction Kaunitz wrote to Berlin, repudiating officially all idea of partition, and declaring that the Empress was ready to give up all the territory which she had occupied in Poland, if other Powers would do the same. In spite of this, there were indications of wavering at the Austrian Court. The Empress's son, Joseph, already elected Emperor of Germany, and who was co-regent with his mother in Hungary, held very different views, and was ready for a deal with Prussia. He was young, but full of ambition, scheming, artful, very modern in many of his political views, opposed to clericalism and feudalism, and very zealous for the improvement of the condition of his people, but most rash and ill-judged in the execution of his schemes. He was passionately in favour of

* Sorel, p. 198.

centralization, greedy for fresh acquisitions of territory, like all his race, and without any scruples. It is probable that Frederick persuaded him to his scheme by judicious flattery, at meetings in 1769 and 1770. Kaunitz also began to waver. Possibly he thought it well to side with the rising sun. At all events, Frederick did not despair of getting the consent of Austria. He made every effort, therefore, to bring his long negotiation with the Empress Catherine to a conclusion.

Meanwhile, there was much discussion between Russia and Prussia as to the details of the partition, and the extent of territory to be acquired by them. Frederick gave way on the subject of Danzig and Thorn. But with these exceptions he insisted upon the whole of West Prussia. Writing to his brother Henry, he said: "As to the Duchy of Wormie" (which he had occupied with his troops), "it is not worth the candle. It is so small that it will not compensate for the clamour it would raise. But Prussian Poland would be worth the trouble, even if Danzig were not included, for we should have the Vistula and free communication with Royal Prussia. . . . When we take a *bagatelle* with *empressement*, a character of avidity and insatiability is given to the transaction, which I do not wish to be attributed to me by Europe more than is already the case."* *Si peccas pecca fortiter* was one of the maxims in politics of this great man. "The command of the Vistula," he added, "will necessarily lead to the acquisition of Danzig at some future time."

Agreement was ultimately arrived at, and on January 15, 1772, two conventions were signed at St. Petersburg by Panine and Solms, on behalf of their respective Governments. By the first of these the Empress of Russia and the King of Prussia, "considering the general confusion in which the republic of Poland exists by the dissension of its leading men, and the perversity of all its citizens," declared the necessity of uniting to their States certain districts of that country, and they promised to support one another in the event of opposition. By the second they regulated the respective aids to one another, and invited the Empress of Austria to join in their scheme.

When the scheme, thus formulated, was presented to the Empress at Vienna she again raised great objections to it. Writing to Kaunitz on the subject, she said that "it will be well not

* Sorel, p. 141.

to lose reputation before God and man by so mean a profit. . . . Right is not on my side—my engagements and equity and common sense are against me. What will all other Powers think of us when they see us losing our reputation for so small a gain?"

Her son, Joseph, and Kaunitz renewed their pressure. They represented to her that her refusal to assent would not prevent Russia and Prussia from prosecuting their scheme of partition, that it could only be prevented by war, and that war would be avoided if Austria was a party to the transaction, and that much bloodshed would be spared if she gave her consent. It was a case with the Empress of "saying she would ne'er consent, consented." She yielded at last to their persuasions, but in so doing she put on record her objections :—

"*Placet*—since so many great and learned men will have it so, but long after I am dead it will be known what this violation of all that we have hitherto held sacred and just will give rise to."

On February 19, 1772, the Empress gave her formal consent to the scheme of partition of Poland, subject to the condition that the shares of the three Powers concerned should be absolutely equal, and that, for the present, the transaction should be kept secret.

The partition, therefore, was agreed to in principle, and there remained only to decide on the parts of Poland to be assigned to each of the three Powers. In the meantime Russia had occupied two-thirds of that country by her troops, and the Austrians and Prussians had advanced their sanitary cordons, so as to encircle the greater part of the territories that each of them wished to acquire. It was not till the end of July that the details of the partition were agreed upon. There was much haggling on the subject. Austria, which had been so loath to come in, was now eager to get the best of the bargain, and had to be restrained by the other two Powers. "Permit me to say," said Frederick to the Austrian Ambassador, "that your mistress has a very good appetite," * and Panine, at St. Petersburg, complained that the proposals of Austria would lead to the complete destruction of Poland. He pointed out that it was not advisable to take too much from Poland. "Poland," he said, "must remain for ever as an intermediary State destined to prevent collision between her three neigh-

* Sorel, p. 218.

bours. We should therefore leave to it a force and existence suitable for such a destination." *

By the treaty thus signed—the preamble to which asserted that it was effected "in the name of the Holy Trinity"—Russia was to have the palatinates of Polock, Witesk, and Mscislaw, as far as the Rivers Dwina and Dneiper, contiguous to her north-western frontier, and consisting of more than 3,000 square leagues. Austria was to have a part of Galicia and a portion of Podolia and Little Poland as far as the Vistula, about 2,500 square leagues. Prussia was to have Polish Prussia (except the towns of Danzig and Thorn with their territories) or about 900 square leagues. The three shares were unequal in area, but did not differ much in population. They formed about one-fourth of the whole kingdom of Poland. The treaty provided that the residue of three-fourths was to remain as a reconstituted Poland, guaranteed by the Powers, under its old anarchical Constitution, which was now made obligatory upon it. The treaty thus effected was kept a profound secret. Kaunitz, when questioned about it by the British Government, denied absolutely that any such treaty existed, or that partition was contemplated. It was not

* Ibid., p. 219.

till September that its contents were made public by the three Powers concerned. They thought it necessary to vindicate this extraordinary and nefarious transaction before the public opinion of Europe by manifestos justifying their actions.

All three put forward ancient claims to the territories now forcibly taken. These claims were dished up for the occasion by the Chancelleries of the respective Courts. They were not worth the paper on which they were written. Their only effect was to show how little could be alleged in favour of the transactions. Poland had been in unquestioned possession of these territories for upwards of two hundred years.

Russia prefaced her spurious claim by setting forth the kindness she had shown to the republic by causing the election of Stanislaus as its King. "That event was necessary to restore the Polish liberty in its ancient lustre, to ensure the elective right of the monarchy, and to destroy foreign influence, which was so rooted in the State and which was the continual source of trouble and contest." She had taken, it was said, far less territory than she was entitled to. In respect of this difference, consisting of territory 50 versts in breadth along the frontier of Poland, "it is a pledge which Russia advances for the solidity of peace which ought to be restored to her when the object of it is effected."

This seemed to point to yet another dismemberment in the near future. The language of Austria pointed in the same direction. After propounding the ancient claim of Hungary, she asked credit for confining herself to a very moderate equivalent for her real pretensions to the best provinces of Poland, such as Podolia, etc.

Prussia also, in unctuous language, said: "We trust that the Polish nation will eventually recover from its prejudices, that it will acknowledge the enormous injustice which it has done to the House of Brandenburg, and that it will bring itself to repair it by a just and honourable arrangement."

Besides these separate vindications, the three Courts issued a joint manifesto on September 26, 1772, in which, after adverting to the part they had taken in the election of Stanislaus, they said:—

"Everything seemed to promise to Poland and her neighbours a firm and lasting tranquillity. But, unhappily, the spirit of discord seized upon one part of the nation, and citizen armed against citizen. Law, order, and public safety, justice, police, commerce, and agriculture, all are either going to ruin or stand on the brink of destruction. Excesses of every kind, the natural consequence of such an anarchy, will bring on the total dissolution of the State if not timely prevented."

They then proceeded to state why the Powers were obliged by this state of anarchy to secure the tranquillity of their own borders. They were exposed to the uncertain but possible consequences of the entire dissolution of Poland. They also referred to their respective claims of right to the territories dealt with, and added that "having communicated reciprocally their rights and claims, and being mutually convinced of the justice thereof, they are determined to secure to themselves a proportional equivalent, by taking immediate and effectual possession of such parts of the territory of the republic as may serve to fix more natural and sure bonds between her and the three Powers."

Stanislaus, with the support of his Ministers, replied to this by a counter-manifesto, basing the right of Poland to the territory seized by the three Powers, on actual possession of over two hundred years. He declared in the most solemn manner that he looked upon the actual seizure of the provinces of Poland as unjust, violent, and contrary to his lawful rights. He appealed to the treaties guaranteeing his kingdom.

Austria, on behalf of the three Powers, replied: "The Empress has seen with unspeakable astonishment the little impression made by the declaration presented to his Polish Majesty by the three Courts as to the pretensions forced by the Powers on Poland. . . . The justice and dignity of the three Courts prescribe bounds to their moderation; the truth can neither escape the discernment of his Polish Majesty nor be indifferent to his heart." "The Empress," it added, "hopes that the King of Poland will not expose his kingdom to events which must be the consequence of his delay to assemble a Diet, but will enter upon a negotiation which alone can save his country. . . ."

Upon receipt of this Stanislaus climbed down, and agreed to summon a Diet. The three Powers had set their hearts upon having their scheme of plunder ratified by the Diet of the unfortunate Poland. The Diet was called on April 10, 1773. Foreign troops were in possession of the whole country. Warsaw was held by Russian, Austrian, and Prussian troops. The three Powers declared that every Deputy who voted against their scheme of partition would be treated as an enemy. Frederick, in his Memoirs, admits that the Diet was informed that if the scheme submitted to them was not adopted, the whole of Poland would be dismembered, but that, if passed, the foreign troops would be withdrawn from the territory it was proposed to leave to the republic. The Diet was confederated, so that the Liberum Veto did not apply, and the majority of its votes prevailed. Immense sums were spent in bribery. A common fund for this purpose was raised by the three Powers. In spite of all these efforts, there was vehement opposition in the Diet. Many strong speeches were made against the scheme. It was not till August 5th that the Diet decided to ratify the treaty. They also agreed at the dictation of Russia to appoint a permanent Council in whom the executive powers were to be vested. The King remained the nominal head, but all real authority was to be exercised by the Russian Ambassador.

The first partition of Poland was now complete. The three Powers were already in possession of the territories agreed upon. It will be seen that this violent act led, by inevitable logic, within a very few years, to the further partition by the same Powers, and to the complete destruction of Poland as a nation. It may be well, therefore, to consider where the responsibility lay for this first transaction.

Frederick the Great has given a defence of his own share in it. Writing to Voltaire on October 9, 1773, he said:—

"To return to your King of Poland. I am aware that Europe pretty generally believes the late partition made of Poland to be a result of the political trickeries which are attributed to me. Nevertheless, nothing is more untrue. After in vain proposing difficult arrangements and expedients, there was no alternative left but either that some partition be made or else Europe hustled into a general war. Appearances are deceitful, and the public judges only by them. What I tell you is as true as the forty-seventh of Euclid."

Voltaire highly approved and applauded the partition. He differed wholly, in this respect, from his contemporary Rousseau, whose influence had great effect in directing the sympathy of democratic Europe against the scheme.* Voltaire

* It should be recollected that Voltaire was in receipt of a pension from Frederick. Rousseau, though a very poor man, declined a most modest offer of alimony from the same quarter. Among the works of Rousseau there is an interesting and sympathetic treatise on Poland, written just before the first partition (*Œuvres de Rousseau*, v. p. 273).

was evidently not impressed by the disclaimer of his correspondent. In a letter to the King on November 16th he wrote: "People assert that it is you who conceived the partition of Poland. I believe it, because there is genius in it, and the treaty was made at Berlin," and again in another letter: "I predicted thirty years ago that you would do great things; but my prediction did not go so far as your acts. It is your destiny always to astonish the world. I know not where you will stop, but I know that the Prussian eagle will go very far." He also expressed his joy that he had lived to see so glorious an event.*

Frederick replied in a letter of December 6th: "I know nothing of treaties signed at Potsdam. I know what has been done at Petersburg. The public, deceived by gazetteers, often does honour to persons in respect of matters in which they have taken no concern." It is evident from this correspondence that Frederick was anxious to escape from the odium which he feared would attach to this transaction.

Carlyle, the eminent historian and biographer of Frederick, accepts these disclaimers, and is at great pains to prove that his hero was not

* *Œuvres de Voltaire*, xxiv. p. 93.

responsible for originating the partition scheme, or even for mainly carrying it into effect.

"Considerable obloquy," says the historian, "still rests on Frederick in many Liberal circles for the partition of Poland. Two things, however, seem to be tolerably clear, though not yet known in Liberal circles: first, that the partition of Poland was an event inevitable in Polish history; an operation of Almighty providence and of the eternal laws of Nature; . . . and, secondly, that Frederick had nothing special to do with it, in the way of originating or causing it—nothing whatever. It is certain the demands of eternal justice must be fulfilled. . . . If the laws and judgments are verily those of God, there can be no clearer merit than that of pushing them forward, regardless of the barkings of gazetteers and wayside dogs. . . . Frederick, in regard to Poland, I cannot find to have anything considerable either of merit or demerit in the moral point of view; but simply to have accepted and put in his pocket without question what Providence sent." *

On the general question of the responsibility of the Poles for their own undoing in respect of the anarchy and misgovernment of their country and the dispensation of Providence in punishment of their crimes, Carlyle has followed Sybel and other German historians in their endeavours to find excuses for the conduct of Prussia. We will deal with this subject later, when commenting on the whole series of partitions which completed the extinction of Poland.

* Carlyle, vi. p. 481.

Meanwhile, it is well to point out that Sybel comes to an opposite conclusion as to the responsibility of Frederick for originating the scheme of the first partition. "The first official suggestion," he says, "came from Prussia. If it had not been made Poland would have remained undivided." *

Sorel also, writing later, with fuller knowledge of all the negotiations, and of the diplomatic records of the three Courts, than probably was possible to Carlyle, comes to the same conclusion. With respect to responsibility for carrying the scheme through all its maze of difficulty, Frederick himself admits it in his Memoirs, where he claims that he gained Poland by "negotiation and intrigue." Carlyle, also, in another passage, practically agrees with this.

"Scrupulous regard to Poland, consideration and magnanimity to her, or the least respect or pity for her as a decaying monarchy is what nobody will claim for Frederick; consummate talent in executing the partition of Poland (inevitable as he may have thought, but is nowhere at the pains to say), great talent, great patience too, and meritorious self-denial, and endeavours in executing that partition, and in saving it from catching fire instead of being the means to quench fire, no well-informed person will deny him." †

---

* Sybel (English translation), ii. p. 347.

† Carlyle, vi. p. 477.

No one, we think, who carefully examines the whole of the negotiations of this period, can come to any other conclusion than that Frederick was responsible for the initiation of the scheme of partition; that its accomplishment was mainly, if not solely, due to his long and arduous efforts; and that his object was not the maintenance of peace, but the acquisition of territory which he held to be vital to the interests of Prussia.

There can be no doubt that this first partition created a most painful impression on Europe. "It is difficult," says Lecky, in a passage which adequately expresses this feeling, "to exaggerate the extent to which the partition (that of 1772) shook the political system, lowered the public morals, and weakened the public law of Europe. It was an example of strong Powers conspiring to plunder a feeble Power, with no more regard for honour or honesty, or the mere decency of appearances, than is shown by a burglar or a footpad." *

* Lecky, *History of England*, v. p. 217.

CHAPTER III

REFORM OF THE POLISH CONSTITUTION

AFTER the partition of 1772, there was a respite to Poland of a few years, and its history during this time is a blank. Though it had lost about one-fourth of its territory, it still retained an important position among European States—a third in the list, in respect of its area, and a fifth in population. The Austrian and Prussian troops were withdrawn from it, in accord with the promises which had been made; but the Russian Government continued to exercise a commanding influence over its administration. Stanislaus was more or less of a cipher, without influence or respect with the Polish people. The anarchic condition of the Constitution, the maintenance of which had been insisted upon by Russia and Prussia, with the express object of keeping Poland in a state of weakness and subservience, prevented any measures for the improvement of the conditions of its population or for strengthening it against external enemies. Death had been busy in the interval since 1772. Frederick the Great died in 1786, and was succeeded by his nephew, Frederick William, a very weak and incompetent personage, compared with his predecessor. Maria Theresa died in 1780, and was succeeded by her son, Joseph II, who, fortunately for his country, came to his end in 1790, and was followed on the throne by his brother, Leopold, a far more sagacious ruler. Of the chief actors in the first partition there remained only the Empress Catherine and the phantom King, Stanislaus, to take part in the measures for the final destruction of Poland as a nation in 1793-5.

In 1788, a wave of patriotic enthusiasm spread over Poland. There was a general sense of humiliation at the impotence to which their country had been reduced. The movement was, to some extent, in sympathy with the democratic principles which were soon to burst into activity in France. But it had little in common with the extreme opinions which eventually obtained control of the National Assembly in Paris.

It was decided, with the assent of King Stanislaus, to summon a Diet at Warsaw, specially for the purpose of amending the Constitution, chiefly in the direction of consolidating the nation, and giving to it an Executive capable of preserving order at home, and of using the resources of the country against external foes.

The Diet, when it assembled on October 6, 1788, confederated itself, so as to relieve its proceedings from the intolerable incubus of the Liberum Veto. Early in its proceedings it showed a strong and patriotic aversion to Russian influence. It abolished the permanent Council appointed in 1773, by which the domination of that Power was mainly secured. It insisted on the withdrawal of all Russian troops from the country. It then proceeded to discuss the details of a scheme for the reform of the Constitution. Nearly four years were spent in protracted and endless discussions. The scheme was vehemently opposed and obstructed by a small minority, consisting in part of great landowners, who were alarmed lest their privileges should be interfered with by a reformed Diet, and in part by others subsidized by the Russian Government. The Diet was legally elected only for two years. At the end of this time new elections took place. But the nuncios elected were added to those of the previous elections. The Diet was thus doubled in number, and its loquacious proceedings were proportionally protracted.

A conclusion of these interminable discussions was only arrived at by a closure of the debates, in the form of a *coup d'état*, arranged between the leaders of the Diet and the King. On May 3, 1791, when the Diet met, the building was surrounded by an immense concourse of people, and its approaches were lined by Polish troops. The Marshal of the Diet opened proceedings by a report, which had been prepared by the Committee on Foreign Affairs. It pointed out the perils of the State caused by the long delay in effecting the necessary reforms. On concluding his report he turned to the King, who was present, and said: "It is your duty, Sire, to prepare measures which will provide means for saving the State." Stanislaus thereupon produced a cut-and-dried scheme of reform prepared by a Committee of Patriots.

After seven hours of heated discussion, the scheme was voted *en bloc* by acclamation, only twelve members observing a gloomy silence. The King thereupon made formal attestation by oath to maintain and observe the new law. He then invited the members of the Diet to follow him to the cathedral, and there swear fidelity to the new Constitution. They did so in a dignified procession, in the presence of vast numbers of the people. Throughout these proceedings Stanislaus acted, for the first and only time in his reign, with dignity and a due sense of patriotism. The Diet placed at the head of their Act of Reform the words, used under similar circumstances, by the National Assembly of France: "All power in a State emanates from the will of the nation."

The Constitution, thus adopted, provided that the throne of Poland should in future be hereditary, and after the death of the reigning King should pass to the Elector of Saxony and his heirs. The Liberum Veto and the right or custom of confederation were abolished, "as contrary to the spirit of the Constitution and as tending to trouble the State." A majority of the Diet was to prevail. The powers of the Provincial Dietines were curtailed. The Diet in future was to consist of two Chambers. The King was to have a suspensory veto only till another Diet had been elected. He was to govern with the aid of six Ministers responsible to the Diet. He was to command the army and to make appointments. The burghers of the towns, hitherto unrepresented, were to be admitted to the franchise, and were to elect members to sit beside those of the ruling class of nobles. The Roman Catholic religion was to be the Established Church, with a tolerance for other sects, but with a prohibition against conversion from one sect to another. The financial system was thoroughly revised. Though the peasant cultivators of the soil were not enfranchised, some improvement in their condition was provided for. The army was to consist of 100,000 men.

There can be no doubt that the Constitution thus enacted by the Diet was approved by an overwhelming majority of the people of Poland. It was promulgated amid great popular rejoicing. The Provincial Dietines ratified it. The British Minister at Warsaw reported to Lord Grenville that there was no apparent opposition to the new system, and that the Russian party, so violent a short time since, had totally disappeared.

It will be seen from the brief description of the new Constitution that it was but a very small step in the direction of democracy. It was an effort to evolve order out of the anarchic chaos, into which the system of government of Poland had fallen, and to consolidate its nationality. As such it was hailed with enthusiasm by many of the best thinkers in Europe, and, among others, by Edmund Burke, who, much as he hated the Revolution in France, had nothing but praise for that in Poland. "Humanity," he wrote, "must rejoice and glory when it considers the change in Poland." Congratulations poured in on Stanislaus from all parts of the world, even from the Vatican.

It has been shown that it had, for years past, been the deliberate policy of Russia to favour and promote anarchy in Poland, and to prevent any reform of its Constitution, or consolidation of the State. The Empress looked on whilst these reforms were being discussed and decided on by the Polish Diet with malevolence and contempt. She held that Stanislaus was personally a traitor to herself, and she was determined to humiliate him, and to destroy the Constitution, which she regarded as a defiance to Russia. During the four years, however, of discussion in the Polish

Diet, Russia was engaged in war with Turkey and Sweden, and was consequently unable to give effective attention to the Polish question, at all events, to an extent that might lead to the use of force. But the Empress endeavoured to keep alive her influence there by intrigues with the small body of nobles who opposed the Constitution, and she disbursed large sums of money in bribery for this purpose.

The King of Prussia, Frederick William, on his part, though quite ready, as the sequel showed, to join in making another grab at Polish territory, had found it to his interest to adjourn his predatory intentions, and to make use of Poland in the prosecution of a new policy. In 1788, while the new Constitution was under discussion by the Polish Diet, he bethought himself that the support of Poland might be useful to him in a war which, in concert with the maritime Powers Great Britain and Holland, he contemplated against Russia, for the purpose of preventing the extension of that Power, on the coasts of the Black Sea, at the expense of Turkey. With the object, therefore, and, at all events, with the hope of detaching Poland from Russia, he offered a close alliance to its Government.

Long delays occurred in discussing the details of agreement, and it was not till March 29, 1790, that a formal treaty was signed, under which Prussia guaranteed its integrity to Poland in the most solemn way, and gave distinct promise of support against any attack upon it from any quarter. It recognized the right of the Poles to revise their Constitution. The King of Prussia further intimated his approval of the scheme of reform of the Constitution, and especially the proposal to make the throne of Poland hereditary, and he promised to use his influence, with the Elector of Saxony, to induce him to accept it after the demise of its present king, Stanislaus.

This treaty between Prussia and Poland, which was so distinctly aimed at the Russian predominance, was gall and wormwood to the Empress Catherine. She determined, without loss of time, to do her best to destroy the new Constitution, and to reduce Poland again to a condition of impotence, subservient to the will of Russia. She decided, therefore, to bring the war with Turkey to an end as soon as possible, so as to free her hands for dealing effectively with the Polish question. Not content with reducing Poland to a vassal

State, she also made up her mind to annex, as a Russian province, another large part of its territory.

It was not till August 11, 1791, that the Empress was able to extricate herself from the war with Turkey. She then came to preliminary terms of peace with the Sultan at Galatz. For this purpose she gave up, for the time being, the greater part of her ambitious scheme of extension of her Empire at the expense of the Turks. She contented herself, on the suggestion of the British Government, with the acquisition of Otchakoff, on the Black Sea, which had been so nearly the cause of war with England, and a district of Bessarabia between the Dneister and the Bourg. She determined to direct her armies, thus liberated, towards Poland, and to make whatever acquisitions of territory were possible on her western frontier, in preference to those on the south.

For this purpose Catherine felt that she could not gain her objects against the opposition of both Austria and Prussia. Indeed, the assistance and co-operation of one or other was expedient, if not absolutely necessary to her. But in such case she would have to admit the co-operator to a share in the plunder. If both of them were unable, through being engaged in operations elsewhere, to oppose her scheme in Poland, she would be able without difficulty to accomplish her purpose alone. She formed, therefore, the most cynical design of embroiling these two Powers in war with France, and when they were fully engaged with their armies in that quarter, to avail herself of the opportunity of seizing for herself alone just so much of Polish territory as she wished for. Circumstances greatly favoured her in this respect; for in 1791 the Revolution in France had reached a point, when the neighbouring Powers were greatly afraid of the extension of its principles among their own subjects, and when the Royal Family of France were appealing to their fellow monarchs in Europe for protection to their persons, and for the restoration of the monarchical system in France, and all its attendant institutions and abuses. This cynical intention of the astute Empress has only been revealed to us of late years through her correspondence. In a letter, dated June 21, 1791, to Professor Grimm, one of the able philosophers, with whom she was in communication, she fully explained her policy.

"I am breaking my head," she wrote, "to make the Cabinets of Vienna and Berlin intervene in the affairs of France. I wish to see them plunged in some very complicated question in order to have my hands free. I have so many enterprises unfinished. . . . It is necessary that these two Courts should be occupied in order that they may not prevent me from bringing them to a good end."

In pursuance of this scheme of policy, Catherine affected to be deeply concerned by the revolutionary movement in France, and eager to form a coalition of European Powers, for the purpose of maintaining the monarchy in France, restoring its arbitrary powers, and suppressing the Revolution. Although it may be that she had much personal sympathy for the Royal Family of France, and that she hated the Revolution, it is now certain, from her subsequent proceedings, that she never had the smallest intention to involve her own country in any active measures of force against France, or to expend a drop of Russian blood, on behalf of the unfortunate French King and his family. The French Revolution was merely a pretext and a diversion to her. Her main, if not sole, object was the acquisition of Poland.

With this object, she accused the Polish patriots of being animated by the same revolutionary principles as the republican party in France. She justified her predatory intentions against Poland, on the ground that it was for the purpose of defeating the inroad of revolutionary principles, and that by destroying them in that quarter, she was taking a part with the other monarchs of Europe in stemming the advance of democracy, and saving their thrones.

It was not, however, till the definitive conclusion of peace with Turkey, in January 1792, that she was able to give effect to her ambitious projects. She then gave immediate orders to her army to advance towards the frontier of Poland. In a letter to her chief Minister, Markoff, she said, with reference to Austria and Prussia: "If they oppose me, I will propose to them either an indemnity or a partition."

In the meantime, in spite of the opposition of Russia, and its subsidized partisans in Poland, the new Constitution of that country, already explained, had been promulgated on May 3, 1791. It was then presented to the Prussian Government, and their approval and support were asked for. The Ministers of Frederick

William, we now know, were strongly opposed to the new Polish Constitution. They drew up a formal report against it for the King. Their principal objection was to the proposal to make the throne of Poland hereditary, and to confer it, after the demise of Stanislaus, on the Elector of Saxony. They represented that the interests of Prussia would be greatly imperilled by a Poland, thus magnified by the addition of Saxony, with an aggregate population of eleven millions, compared with that of Prussia of six millions only. A State with this population, almost wholly Catholic, wedged in between Austria and Prussia, would fall under the influence of one or other of them. There would be no security for Prussia, they said, unless Poland continued to be a freely elective monarchy. In spite of this report from his recognized Ministers, Frederick William, acting on the advice of others in the background, as was often his wont, decided against them, and on May 8th expressed to the Polish Ambassador his cordial approval of the new Constitution, and of the proposed offer of the throne to the Elector of Saxony. He directed that assurance to this effect should be conveyed to Warsaw. He professed himself fully determined to fulfil his treaty obligations to Poland. In a personal letter to Stanislaus, dated May 23rd, he wrote: "I congratulate myself on having had it in my power to maintain the liberty and independence of the Polish nation, and one of my most pleasing cares will be to support and draw closer the bond which unites us." * He also wrote to the Elector of Saxony urging him to accept the reversion to the throne of Poland.

On this transaction Sybel the historian and apologist of Prussia observes :—

> "Every lover of Prussia must regret that the Report of the Ministry did not receive the Royal Assent, and that Prussia did not, in the face of all the world, renounce the treaty with Poland. It was beyond all question that no alliance was possible between Prussia and a firmly established Poland, and the longer the open acknowledgment of this fact was delayed the greater was the danger to Prussia of bringing upon herself the charge of utter perfidy."

The passage is important, for it shows that in the opinion of this patriotic German the conduct of the King of Prussia in this matter laid him open to the charge of utter perfidy.

When this action of the King is compared with his subsequent course in the abandon-

* Fletcher's *Poland*, p. 204.

ment of Poland a few months later and his taking part in her dismemberment, it can only be concluded that he deliberately deceived the Polish Government, and that he fully intended to reverse his policy at the earliest possible moment. The fact was that at the time when these assurances were given by the King of Prussia, the war of Russia with Turkey had not yet been brought to a conclusion. There was still a possibility of Prussia being drawn into it against Russia. It doubtless seemed to the Prussian King a dangerous policy to alienate Poland, at such a time, and thus perhaps to drive her into the arms of Russia. By his readiness to accede to the wishes of Poland, as regards her new Constitution, he might count on her assistance, if Russia should drive matters to extremity. He had detached Poland from her ancient alliance, or rather it should be called subjection, to Russia. He must have known that his support was equally important to Poland for the maintenance of the new Constitution, as against the intrigues of Russia.

No sooner was the fear of all danger from war with Russia removed, than there were strong indications of an intention, on the part of

Frederick William, to take part in another scheme for dismembering his ally. The first suggestion of this was a proposal on the part of Prussia to the Polish Government to give up to her the towns of Danzig and Thorn, in return for a favourable commercial treaty. The population of these two towns, and the districts around them, was German in race, and it was no doubt of considerable importance to Prussia that they should be incorporated in her dominion. They formed "enclaves" surrounded by districts, which had been made over to Prussia, under the partition scheme of 1772. The British Government was favourable to the Prussian demand, and advised the Poles to accede to it. But Danzig was the only access of Poland to the sea. The proposal met with a fierce and patriotic opposition on the part of the Poles. It was withdrawn by the Prussian Government. But very soon there were indications of the abandonment by Prussia of its pledges of support, and of its intention to join in a scheme of plunder at the expense of Poland.

CHAPTER IV

COALITION AGAINST FRANCE

OTHER events of importance were now occurring in Europe which delayed the attack on Poland, and which for a time seemed to offer to her some hope of support against Russia. The Revolution in France was running its course and was becoming more violent. Louis XVI and Marie Antoinette, in fear for their lives, and despairing of the monarchy, without the assistance of foreign countries, made desperate appeals to their brother monarchs in Europe to assist them. They had special claims on the Queen's brother, the Emperor of Austria. Their fate interested Frederick William also much more than his Ministers. It was the cause of a *rapprochement* between the Courts of Austria and Prussia. Much discussion took place between them as to armed intervention in France. The Emperor of Austria, Leopold, was very averse to intervention if it could possibly be averted, as was also his chief

Minister, Prince Kaunitz. The Emperor recognized his obligation to his sister, but he strongly advised her and Louis, her husband, to come to terms with the National Assembly, and he hoped in this way to avoid the necessity for intervention.

The King of Prussia, on his part, was far more eager to intervene in France. He was personally alarmed by the course of events there. His Ministers were much less disposed to war than himself. The King, however, admitted that war, for the purpose of saving the French monarchy, could only be carried on by a coalition, and that, singly, it was impossible for him to undertake it. Negotiations, therefore, for this purpose were entered into with Austria. The discussion between the two Powers brought the question of Poland to the front. It was obviously impossible to engage in a policy of war with France without having come to agreement about Poland. An agreement was eventually arrived at on July 25, 1791, which some months later, in February 1792, was embodied in a formal treaty. It was decided that neither of them should undertake anything against the territorial status of Poland, or against its free

Constitution. They mutually guaranteed their present possessions, and agreed to afford assistance to one another, in the event of any internal disturbance of their respective States. They also agreed to lose no time in promoting a concert of European Powers in support of the French monarchy.

In pursuance of this undertaking a further meeting took place between the Emperor and Frederick William, at Pilnitz in Saxony, on August 25, 1791, for the purpose of deciding what active measures should be taken against France. The meeting was attended by the Comte D'Artois, brother of Louis XVI, who represented the views of the French *émigrés*, and passionately urged intervention to put down the Revolution in France, and to restore the *ancien régime*. The two sovereigns were not impressed by him. They decided that intervention in France should not be attempted, without the combined support of other European Powers. They proposed to invite the co-operation of all European Powers, and if that were attained "*alors et dans ce cas*" there should be active intervention on their part. All action, therefore, on the part of the two Powers most immediately concerned, was to be absolutely conditional upon the co-operation of other Powers, and as it was known for certain that England, at that time, had no intention whatever of being drawn into war with France, the result of the meeting was the defeat, for the time being, of the war party, and their whole policy of intervention in France. The Emperor, whose views thus prevailed, wrote to Kaunitz that he might be quite easy in his mind as he, Leopold, had evaded all binding engagements for war with France. "*Alors et dans ce cas*," he said, "is with me the Law and the Prophets."

It followed from these proceedings between the two German Powers that the war with France was averted, and that the machinations of Catherine were foiled. With regard to Poland also, the Powers were ostensibly in agreement to respect its territory, and its new Constitution, and to support the proposal of the Polish Diet to make the throne of that country hereditary in the line of the Saxon Royal Family. They agreed to advise the Elector of Saxony to accept the offer of the throne of Poland.

The value of these engagements between the two monarchs, however, was already discounted, in the knowledge of the British Government, for it appears that in August of this year Ewart, the British Minister at Berlin, reported to Lord Grenville a conversation with Count Schulenburg, the Prussian Minister who had succeeded Count Hertsberg in July. Schulenburg, he said, expressed himself as gratified that Austria had guaranteed the integrity of Poland; but he asserted the belief that this would be of little use against the ambitions of Russia; that the Emperor, finding it impossible to stop the ambitions of Russia, would be compelled to participate in some plan for another partition of Poland; and that his own Government, Prussia, would be unable to avoid joining in it, even without the implication of Austria.* This was the first official hint of a second partition, which was so soon to be effected by Russia and Prussia.

The meeting at Pilnitz took place shortly after the forced return of Louis XVI and his family from Varennes. There followed, three months later, the acceptance by the King of the Constitution, which had been elaborated by the Constituent Assembly of France. The King announced his acceptance to his brothers. The Queen did the same to her brother, the Emperor, in a letter prepared for her by Barnave, and

* Ewart to Grenville, August 4, 1791. Record Office.

the leaders of the Constitutional party in the Assembly. The Emperor accepted this as the genuine expression of the intention of the King and Queen. He was determined, if possible, to avoid being drawn into war with France. He took no notice therefore of another letter of Marie Antoinette, written the very next day, in which she protested that her previous letter did not express her real views, but the very contrary; and in which she urged on him the extreme importance of armed intervention, for the purpose of saving the lives of the Royal Family, and of putting down the Revolution.

Although the meeting at Pilnitz, and the consequent declarations of Austria and Prussia, resulted, as the Emperor intended, in averting war for a time, the menacing words used in them against the Revolution were taken by the National Assembly in Paris, and by the French people, as a declaration of enmity, and a determination to destroy the new Constitution, and to restore the power of absolute monarchy, by invasion and war. It was so announced by Comte D'Artois and the French *émigrés*. They filled Europe with rejoicing that the Revolution was doomed. The significance of the equivocal words "*alors et dans ce cas*," though considered by the Emperor sufficient to save the position, was not appreciated in France and elsewhere. The declaration was everywhere considered as a challenge by the two Powers concerned, and as meaning that war was inevitable. It did, therefore, infinite mischief in aggravating the position, and in bringing about that which the Emperor Leopold hoped and intended to avoid.

In the atuumn of 1791 everything which occurred tended to war. The grave events in Paris, the stormy debates in the Assembly on foreign affairs, and especially against Austria, the action taken against the feudal rights of the German princes in Alsace, and against the Elector of Trèves, in respect of the French *émigrés*, the passionate entreaties of Louis XVI and the Queen for aid, led the Emperor, most unwillingly, to the conclusion that war was inevitable.

In spite of Leopold's distrust of Prussia, negotiations were renewed with that Power, and a formal treaty was concluded on February 7, 1792, in accord with the preliminary agreement already referred to. It mutually guaranteed their possessions, and bound each to come to the assistance of the other, in the event of attack. It contained the provisions as to Poland already referred to, with the difference only that the two Powers agreed to respect "a" free Constitution there, and did not bind themselves to the actual Constitution of 1791. They agreed to invite Russia to undertake not to interfere with the integrity of Poland. In the discussions which preceded this treaty there was much said about indemnities to meet the expenses of war with France. It was suggested that Prussia should find compensation in Juliers and Berg, Austria in Alsace and Lorraine. The Emperor, however, declined to go into detail. As regards Poland, there was serious divergence of views. The Emperor wished to preserve its integrity. Frederick William indicated a preference for another partition. Leopold proposed an *entente* with Russia, with a view to its neutralization; Frederick William inclined to approach Catherine, with a view to both Powers obtaining a share in a new dismemberment. The Emperor avoided committal. The treaty as signed maintained the original intention that the two Powers should respect the integrity of Poland, and a free Constitution for it.

Sir Morton Eden, the British Ambassador

at Berlin, writing to Lord Grenville on February 16th, made the significant remark: "If the Russian troops invade Poland, and if the Empress proposes a new partition, there will not be wanting plausible reasons for showing the political necessity for participating in it." * He referred especially to Prussia. As regards Austria, there can be no doubt that Leopold was strongly in favour of maintaining the integrity of Poland.

This treaty with Prussia was the last political action of Leopold. He died after four days' illness of smallpox in March 1792. His death was the cause of rejoicing to the war parties at Vienna and Berlin, and still more so to the French *émigrés*. It was a grave misfortune for Poland. Had he lived, the whole course of events which followed might have been different. It was still possible that war with France might have been avoided. He certainly would have done his utmost to prevent the dismemberment of Poland. He was more than a match for Frederick William in the difficult and treacherous mazes of diplomacy.

* Eden to Grenville, February 16, 1792. Record Office.

CHAPTER V

THE PERFIDY OF PRUSSIA

LEOPOLD'S son, Francis, at the early age of twenty-two, succeeded as King of Bohemia and Hungary, and, a few months later, was designated Emperor by the Electors of Germany. He held these honours throughout the long revolutionary wars, and all the great vicissitudes in Austria, during a reign of forty-three years. He was of a very different stamp to his father, who, unfortunately for his country and for Europe, had reigned for only two years. Francis had no political experience, and was of very ordinary intelligence. He was of weak and nervous constitution. He disliked work, and was subject to fits of ennui and depression. Though well-meaning, and with a sense of public duty, he had none of his father's Italian subtlety of mind, and calm and statesmanlike outlook on the whole field of politics. So far as he had formed any political views, they were not in accord with those of his father. He affected great admiration for his uncle Joseph. It will be seen that he soon threw over his father's policy of maintaining the independence of Poland, and, impelled by hereditary craving for territorial aggrandizement, favoured its partition. He had not the same distrust of Prussia, till experience forced it upon him. On the very day of the death of his father he wrote to the King of Prussia, announcing his accession, and expressing the earnest hope that the alliance between the two countries would be cemented. Within a few weeks he committed himself to a policy of war against France in concert with that monarch.

The Empress Catherine, who was ready to invade Poland, and only delayed doing so until Austria and Prussia were engaged in war with France, appears to have taken the measure of the two monarchs, and to have decided to give preference to Frederick William as her partner in the further dismemberment of that country. She directed Suboff, the reigning favourite, a young man of twenty-one years, the latest of her temporary and fleeting consorts, forty years younger than herself, and incompetent for public affairs, to sound the

Prussian Ambassador, Baron Goltz, on the subject. Suboff pointed out the great danger to Prussia of a Poland strengthened by the addition of Saxony. Russia, he said, was disposed to associate Prussia in a new partition of Poland, on condition of the destruction of the new Constitution of 1791, and a restoration of the old one, in what would remain of that kingdom, after its dismemberment. It appears, also, from subsequent proceedings, that it was well understood that the share of the plunder offered was to be conditional on Prussia joining Austria in war against France, the effect of which would be to prevent the armed intervention of Austria in Poland. Frederick William greedily swallowed the bait, and thenceforth forgot his solemn treaty with Poland of 1790, his assurances to that country on the completion of the new Constitution of 1791, and his treaty with Austria, of which the ink was scarcely dry, binding him to maintain the integrity of Poland and a free Constitution for it. All these were mere scraps of paper, of no binding value, as against the interest of Prussia in the accretion of new territory, following in this respect the precepts and example of the great Frederick.

The King, on coming to this decision, wrote to his Ministers, on March 12th, as follows: "Russia is not far removed from thoughts of a new partition, and this would indeed be the most effectual means of limiting the power of a Polish King, whether hereditary or elective. I doubt, however, whether, in this case, a suitable compensation could be found for Austria; and whether, after such a curtailment of the power of Poland, the Elector of Saxony would accept the crown; yet if Austria could be compensated, the Russian plan would be the most advantageous for Prussia. . . . This is my judgment respecting Polish affairs."

Sybel the historian, in quoting this decision of Frederick William, says:—

"This was Poland's sentence of death"; and he adds the following moral, or perhaps we should say casuistical, reflections: "It was not the result of a long-existing greed, but a suddenly devised expedient which seemed to be accompanied with the least evil, in the midst of an unexampled European crisis. I shall leave it out of the question whether it was not possible, under the then existing circumstances, to have acted with more political wisdom; but I doubt whether we can reproach the King, humanly speaking, for acting as he did, in that conflict of duties. One thing is certain, that in this case too the eternal law of justice has been upheld, which demands atonement for every moral delinquency, whatever may be the reasons and excuses urged in palliation, The breach of faith towards Poland, however unavoidable, has been bitterly avenged on Prussia, and that the warning might be the more deeply felt, it was avenged by the hand, not of the victim but of the accomplice in the crime." *

It is difficult to understand what the historian was alluding to, when he alleged that the wrong to Poland was avenged on Prussia by Russia. If he referred to the fact that at the Congress of Vienna, in 1815, the Emperor of Russia insisted on the cession to him of that part of Poland, including the city of Warsaw, which had been acquired by Prussia in 1795, but which had been taken from her by Napoleon in 1807, it should be recollected that Prussia received, at the Congress, an exact equivalent for her Polish province, in a slice of the Kingdom of Saxony, and was perfectly satisfied with the exchange. In any case, it was cold comfort to the Poles that the wrong done to them was avenged on the perpetrators by some other Power, without restitution to them of the territory and the independence of which they had been robbed.

Though war was now decided on by the two Courts of Vienna and Berlin, for the purpose of putting down the Revolution, it was actually

* Sybel, ii. 21.

precipitated by a declaration of hostilities on the part of France against Austria. Meanwhile the question arose as to the indemnities for the expenses of the war.

The Austrian Ambassador at Berlin was sounded by Count Schulenberg, the Prussian Minister, on behalf of Frederick William, as to the possibility of the indemnity to Prussia consisting of the Polish province of Posen. It was suggested that the indemnity to Austria should be the exchange of Belgium for Bavaria, which was well known to have been long the aim of Austria. This, apparently, did not satisfy the Austrian Court. They pressed also for the cession by Prussia of Anspach and Bayreuth, which had recently been made over to Frederick William by their then reigning Prince. This was more than Prussia would concede. The proposal was indignantly rejected. No positive agreement was arrived at as to the indemnities, and this subject continued to be the cause of distrust and jealousy between Austria and Prussia, and, as will be shown, most seriously compromised success in the war, on which they were now embarking as allies. By this time, as we now know, a complete, though secret, understanding was come to between

Russia and Prussia, that in consideration of the latter making war against France, she was to have a share in the plunder of Poland, to consist of the province of Posen and the cities of Danzig and Thorn.

The Empress Catherine, having come to terms with Prussia for a new partition of Poland, when she heard that the two German Powers were determined on war with France, felt that her hands were free, and no longer hesitated as regards her schemes against Poland. It happened, therefore, by a coincidence fatal to that unfortunate country, that almost at the same time, early in April 1792, Austria and Prussia gave orders to their armies to prepare for the invasion of France, and Catherine directed her army to cross the frontier of Poland. The two German Powers were to invade France, for the alleged purpose of putting down the Revolution, and maintaining the Bourbon monarchy in the interest of Europe, but with the ulterior motive of adding to their own dominions, Prussia by a slice of Poland, Austria by securing Bavaria in exchange for Belgium, which had proved to be something of a white elephant to her. Catherine, on her part, invaded Poland ostensibly to destroy the new Constitution, and to set up the old one, but really with the intention of annexing one part of it, as a Russian province, of making a gift of another part to Prussia, and of reducing what would remain of Poland to the position of an impotent vassal State.

Catherine gave orders to two *corps d'armée* to invade Poland, the one from the banks of the Danube, which had been employed against Turkey, the other from the north. She gave notice, at the same time, to Austria and Prussia that she did not intend to be a party to their treaty of February 7th, which stipulated that nothing should be done to interfere with the integrity of Poland, or with the maintenance of a free Constitution for it.

The Polish Diet met, on April 16th, to decide on measures for resisting the Russian invasion. It confided the defence of the country to Stanislaus. It gave him *carte blanche*. But the position was almost hopeless. Of the army of 100,000 contemplated by the Constitution of the previous year, not more than half was in existence. There was no money in the Treasury, and no warlike stores of any kind in the arsenals. In their peril the Polish Government applied to Prussia for assistance, appealing to the treaty of 1790, by which that country guaranteed the integrity of Poland. The answer was given through Lucchesini, the Prussian Minister at Warsaw, the same statesman who had negotiated, on behalf of Prussia, the treaty of 1790. "My master," he replied, on May 4th, "does not consider himself bound by the treaty of 1790 to defend by his army the hereditary monarchy, as established by the Constitution of May 3, 1791." He denied that his Government was bound in any way to assist the Poles under existing circumstances. Further representations were made to the Prussian Government at Berlin, backed up by the British Minister. Sir Morton Eden, in a letter of May 12, 1792, gave a full account of the interview between Count Potocki, the Polish Minister, and Count Schulenberg. The former appealed to the article of the treaty, which expressly stipulated that assistance should be given by Prussia, if any Power, under any pretence, interfered in the internal affairs of Poland. Schulenberg denied that the *casus fœderis* had arisen; for the change, he said, in the Polish Constitution, which had been effected subsequent to the signature of the treaty, and without the privity of the King of Prussia, had essentially altered the political connection of the two countries. Potocki here observed that if his Prussian Majesty's approbation of the revolution, subject to its taking place, were alone wanting to justify the claims of his country to his Majesty's protection, he was willing to rest it on that ground, and immediately produced the copy of the dispatch, dated May 10th of the same year, from his Prussian Majesty himself to Baron Goltz, Chargé d'Affaires at Warsaw. In this dispatch his Prussian Majesty extolled the revolution as likely to strengthen the alliance between the two countries, approved of the choice made of the Elector of Saxony, and expressly enjoined Baron Goltz to communicate the contents to the King of Poland. To this paper the Prussian Minister could oppose nothing except censure of the indiscretion of his Ministry, for having given a copy of it to the Polish Government. Potocki observed very properly that this appeared to him to be immaterial, since a mere verbal assurance by his Prussian Majesty would have been equally obligatory.

A few days later, Eden wrote again that on all sides, at Berlin, the Poles encountered systematic coldness. Hertzberg said that they deserved their fate, because they would not cede Danzig and Thorn. General Möllendorf expressed frankly his opinion of the ruinous folly of a war with France, which left Russia the sole arbiter of the fate of Poland. He added, however, that every Prussian, without exception of party, would agree that their country could never acquiesce in the establishment of a good Government in Poland, since in a very short time it would rise to a very decided superiority. The pretence, however, was still kept up that the question at issue was, not the integrity and independence but only the Constitution of Poland. The Prussian Minister reported that the Empress's views did not extend beyond the overthrow of the new Constitution. But Eden added significantly: "I continue of opinion that if the proposals for a new partition be made, plausible reasons will be found to remove the scruples of his Prussian Majesty."

We now know that when the Prussian Ministers were attempting these explanations to Eden, and to the Polish Minister, their Government had already come to terms with the Empress Catherine to share with her the dismemberment and spoil of Poland. This added to the exceptional perfidy of the whole transaction. Not only did Prussia refuse to give the assistance promised by solemn treaty rather less than two years previously, to prevent the integrity of Poland being interfered with from any quarter, but she was herself in conspiracy with Russia to make the attack, and had agreed to share in the plunder. In the annals of Europe there had been no more shocking and scandalous transaction.

On May 26th, the King of Prussia threw off his mask and issued a manifesto announcing to all the world his intention to invade Great Poland, and assigning as a reason for this treachery, and the disregard of his former treaties, that "the principles of Jacobinism are gaining ground in that country, that the spirit of French democracy and the principles of that atrocious sect, which seeks to make proselytes on all sides, begin to take root in Poland, so that the manœuvres of the Jacobin emissaries are powerfully supported there, and that there are already formed there several revolutionary clubs which make an open profession of their sentiments." He admitted that he had concerted this scheme with the Courts of Vienna and St. Petersburg, and that he intended to incorporate several districts of Great Poland and the towns of Thorn and Danzig. After stating that he had ordered his troops to enter Poland, he proceeded to say: "The King flatters himself that, with feelings so pacific, he may depend on the goodwill of a nation whose welfare can never be indifferent to him, and to which he wishes to give real proofs of his affection and regard." *

There was no better hope for Poland from Austria. "I am not without suspicion," wrote Keith, the British Ambassador at Vienna, on May 12th, "that Austria already knows that Prussia will set up no direct opposition to the Empress Catherine's views, and . . . that a co-operation of the three Powers may renew the former scenes of depredation, and consummate the ruin of the miserable kingdom of Poland." † A week later, May 19th, he wrote: "Austria has not, to my knowledge, consented to any project of dismemberment, but her principles are not of so rigid a stamp as to hinder her coming in (sneakingly) at the hour of partition for such a share of the garment as may suit her views." It will

* Fletcher's *Poland*, p. 312.

† Keith to Grenville, May 12, 1792. Record Office.

be seen later how fully Keith's predictions were verified.

We now know that the Emperor Francis had, by this time, decided to abandon the policy of his father, of maintaining the integrity of Poland, and to revert to that of Joseph II. Though he did not as yet want an addition to his own Polish province, he was ready to agree to Prussia taking an indemnity for the expense of its war with France, by sharing with Russia in the plunder of Poland. For his own indemnity he preferred the annexation of Bavaria to his German territory by way of exchange for Belgium.

This scheme was decided on by the Emperor behind the back of Kaunitz, the chief Minister of his empire. That old and eminent statesman, when the transaction was revealed to him, objected in the strongest terms. "The scheme," he said, "is chimerical. It is unjustifiable so far as Poland is concerned. We cannot honestly dismember the republic, under pretext that it has established a Constitution which it was agreed to respect. . . . It is unacceptable so far as concerns Bavaria. The reigning family there will not consent, and Austria has by the treaty of The Hague renounced the exchange. It is imprudent, for the partition would be unequal Prussia will enter into enjoyment of its share, while Austria will be reduced to hopes and expectations."

His opposition was unavailing. He sent in his resignation of the post he had filled for so many years. It was not accepted for some months, and he continued to be nominally at the head of affairs, but he ceased to exercise any control over them. Baron Cobenzl practically superseded him, on August 19th, as the chief adviser of the Emperor.

Austria, at war with France, had the right, under its treaty with Russia of 1781, renewed as lately as 1789, to appeal to her for assistance. Both Austria and Prussia invited Catherine to support them in their proposed invasion of France, on behalf of its monarchy, and for the purpose of preventing the spread of the Revolution.

Catherine replied to these demands with a delicate irony which did credit to her wit and lightness of touch. "It is well indeed," she wrote to the Emperor Francis, "for a young Sovereign to commence his career by an enterprise which has for its object the preservation of Europe from the contagion of an example so scandalous and baneful. But that which has happened in a country so far removed as France is from my own State, has called my attention to what is occurring in my own neighbourhood. The subversion of the Constitution of Poland, by the new Constitution of May 3, 1791, will produce disorders analogous to those of France." She would occupy herself, she said, in stemming this evil so near at hand. She claimed the right to call upon Austria, under the treaty of 1788, to assist her in this. She recognized that in the difficulties in which Austria was engaged, it could not be expected to do so. She set off the one obligation against the other, and justified in this way her refusal to assist Austria in war against France.

Writing to Grimm about the same time, she said: "You seem to think that the Polish affair is not on the same lines as that of France. You ignore apparently the fact that the Jacobins of Warsaw are in close correspondence with those of Paris. You wish me to neglect the interests of my allies in Poland, in order to occupy myself with the Jacobinism of Paris. No, I will fight the enemy in Poland, and in so doing I shall not the less occupy myself with the affairs of France."

CHAPTER VI

INVASION BY RUSSIA

CATHERINE, it has been already stated, on April 8th, gave orders to her army to invade Poland. It consisted of 80,000 troops of the line and 20,000 Cossacks. It was accompanied by a group of Polish magnates who formed the minority in the Diet which had unsuccessfully opposed the new Constitution. Later they had gone on a deputation to St. Petersburg, with the hope of inducing Catherine to intervene in Poland, for the restoration of the old anarchical system. The Empress made much of them, and promised her support. She affected to treat them as the true representatives of the Polish people. On her suggestion, supported by the Russian army, these few men set up a rival Diet at Targovitz, in Poland, and issued a proclamation, denouncing the Diet of Warsaw as an usurpation, and claiming for themselves that they were the only legal Assembly.

On April 18th Bolgakoff, the Russian Minister at Warsaw, delivered a declaration of war, on the part of Russia, to the King, accompanied by a manifesto of the Empress. It asserted a right and obligation, on the part of Russia, to take part in whatever related to the government and affairs of Poland. It complained in violent terms of the change which had taken place in the Constitution, which it represented as a total subversion of the ancient Polish liberty, and as effected chiefly by partisan violence. It charged the Diet with countenancing opprobrious language respecting the conduct and intentions of herself, the Empress. It asserted the new Government to be a tyranny established against the will of the nation, the most respectable part of which had appealed to the Court of St. Petersburg for protection and a restoration of the former Government. Induced by these motives, it said, the Empress had decided to take an active part on their behalf, and at their request to restore the ancient order of things in Poland, and to treat as enemies all those who should oppose her endeavours to accomplish that object.

Nothing was said in this of the ultimate intention of Catherine to effect a second dismemberment of the kingdom, and to annex a great part of it, as a Russian province, or of her promises to the King of Prussia of a share of the plundered country. The dispute with Poland was treated as having relation only to its new Constitution. On laying this declaration before the Diet, Stanislaus asserted his conviction that the Empress intended not only to subvert the Constitution, but to bring the country and himself under her subjection. He entreated the Diet manfully to support the system which they had adopted. The Diet unanimously supported him, invested him with command of their army, and entrusted him with the full resources of the country. He swore on his part to defend Poland and its Constitution with his life. It was decided to increase the numbers of the Polish army to the 100,000 provided in the Constitution. The nobility of Poland showed great enthusiasm for the national cause. Many of them raised regiments in their districts and provided them with arms and accoutrements. Their efforts, however, were too late. Had these measures been adopted immediately after the establishment of the new Constitution, there might have been good prospects of resisting the invasion.

The existing army consisted of less than 50,000 men, of which more than half were in garrisons, spread over very wide districts. Not more than 20,000 men could be collected to form an army in the field to oppose the Russian invasion. It must be admitted also that there was nothing in the nature of a national rising of all classes, such as there was in France, to offer resistance to the enemy. The peasantry, who formed the vast majority of the population of Poland, were still in the lowest state of serfdom, subject to the uncontrolled rule of their feudal lords. They were inarticulate at this crisis. They were indifferent as to the constitution of the central Government, or whether one Diet or the other should prevail. It was suggested that the great landowners were afraid of the peasants being enrolled as soldiers, lest they should use their arms in an agrarian revolt. But there was no sign of any movement of the peasants, or of their welcoming the Russian invaders. With the exception of Warsaw, there were few large towns where the burghers formed an important class. The army was mainly recruited from the *petite noblesse*, who brought with them horses and arms.

The main Russian army, under General

Kackowski, crossed the Polish frontier on May 18th, and advanced in three columns, each of over 20,000 men. The Polish army, under Prince Poniatowski, the nephew of Stanislaus, equal in force only to one of these divisions, made vigorous efforts to resist the Russians. In several conflicts with one or other of the Russian columns they achieved notable successes. But in every case they soon found themselves outflanked by the other Russian columns, and compelled to retreat. In this way they were driven through Podolia and Volhynia. Another Russian army advanced unopposed, and occupied Wilna, where the Confederation of Targowitz was proclaimed with great military pomp. The Empress wrote under her own hand to Stanislaus, informing him that it was useless for him to make further resistance, as she was determined to double or treble her army, rather than abandon the objects she had in view. She announced that the Austrians and Prussians were in alliance with her, and that further opposition would only have the effect of inducing those Powers to give her more effectual support.

On June 22nd, Stanislaus, who had not left Warsaw, and had not risked his life on behalf of his country, as he had sworn to do, despairing of the position, wrote personally to the Empress Catherine, appealing to their something more than intimate friendship in the past, not so much on his own behalf, for he offered to resign his throne, but on behalf of Poland. "I will speak briefly and frankly," he said. "It is important to you to have influence in Poland, and to keep the line of march open, whether against the Turks or against Europe. It is important to us (the Poles) to bring to a close an endless revolution, and the constant interference of our enemies. We need, moreover, a stronger and better regulated Government than we have hitherto possessed. There are means of uniting all these advantages. Give us your grandson, the Grand Duke Constantine, as our King; give us likewise an eternal alliance and an advantageous treaty of commerce with your country. I will say no more. You need no instruction and no guidance."

The proposal was in conflict with Catherine's engagements to Prussia, and with her own intention to incorporate with Russia a large part of Poland. She replied that the only way in which he could help his country was by giving his immediate support to the Confederation of

Targowitz. It was also more fully explained to Stanislaus by the Russian Minister that the Empress could not recognize the Government which existed at Warsaw, that Russia was not at war with Poland, but was acting on behalf of its legitimate Government, the Confederation of Targowitz. Urgent appeals were made by Stanislaus to Austria. The reply was that the Emperor Francis had no reason to oppose the wishes of Russia.

Applications for aid from France and England were no more successful. Dumouriez, on behalf of the former, replied that France could do nothing. In a debate in the French Assembly, doubt was thrown on the Polish revolution. It was held to be organized only in favour of the aristocracy. The democracy of France had no interest in supporting it. The British Minister at Warsaw was instructed by Lord Grenville to say that his Government was not to hold out any expectation of support to Poland from the maritime Powers, England and Holland, and that "no intervention on their part could be serviceable to Poland, without much greater exertion and expense than the maintenance of their separate interests could possibly justify."

Meanwhile, Kachowski was engaged in advancing with his three columns *en échelon*, and was continually outflanking and outnumbering the Poles. The opposing Polish army was now under the command of Kosciuszko, the patriot whose name is identified with the cause of Poland, more especially in connection with the resistance to the third partition in 1795.

Kosciuszko, born of an ancient Polish family of Lithuania, in 1740, crossed the Atlantic in 1775, and engaged as a volunteer in the American army fighting against Great Britain in the war of independence. He was associated there with Lafayette. He soon gave proof of military capacity. He was selected by General Washington as one of his *aides de camp*, and eventually was nominated as General of a brigade. He returned to Poland in 1783, with a great reputation, and was received with enthusiasm by the citizens of Warsaw. When, ten years later, Russia declared war against Poland, Kosciuszko was appointed second in command of the Polish army. He was the only general with any military experience. He soon showed his great ability, and his dauntless courage. In the face of the overwhelming force of the Russians his efforts were hopeless. After an heroic defence, the Polish army was defeated, on July 17th, at Dubienka, on the River Bug. After this the Russians were able to advance to Warsaw without further opposition.

At a meeting of the Polish Diet, Stanislaus advised them that resistance was no longer possible, and that it only remained for them to submit to the Empress. The Diet, by a large majority, acquiesced, and voted its own dissolution. It recognized the Confederation of Targowitz as the Government of the country. The Constitution of 1791 was annulled; the old one was restored. The army was directed to lay down its arms and surrender to the Russians.

The leaders of the patriots, who had been responsible for the new Constitution, fled the country to Vienna and Dresden. Stanislaus found himself deserted, friendless, and impotent in his palace at Warsaw. He submitted himself to the Empress, and declared his adhesion to the Diet at Targowitz. He ceased, thenceforth, to be of any account. He was despised equally by all parties.

CHAPTER VII

THE SECOND PARTITION (1793)

By the end of July 1792 Poland was completely in the power of Russia. The Empress Catherine had achieved the object of her ambition. Taking advantage of the entanglement of the two German Powers in their war with France, which she had done her best to urge upon them, without disclosing her ultimate designs, she had successfully invaded Poland on the plea that she was bound to maintain its old Constitution against dangerous innovators, imbued with the principles of the French Revolution. The whole of Poland was now at her disposition to do as she willed with it. Her troops in actual occupation treated it as a conquered country.

The Polish army, though not yet disbanded, was everywhere surrounded and overawed by superior numbers of Russian troops. In every part of the country there were requisitions, organized pillage under the pretext of domiciliary visits, and arbitrary arrests. There was terrorism in the towns. In the rural districts the serfs were encouraged to rise against their feudal lords, the châteaux were devastated, and everywhere there were assassinations and incendiarisms. All the horrors of civil war were combined with those of foreign invasion in this unfortunate country.

The Confederation of Targowitz, which pretended to represent the country, had formed an Executive Committee, "the generality," as it was called, for administering the government. It was made to understand that it must do nothing without the consent of its real master, the Russian Government. In fact, orders were issued from St. Petersburg in every detail of administration, and the sham Diet of Targowitz and its "generality" had no power to resist, or to initiate anything.

The Empress had still to decide what should be done with this conquered country. She had come to an understanding with Frederick William that an indemnity for the expenses of the war with France was to be found for Prussia out of Poland, but nothing had been settled as to the extent of territory to be thus assigned. Catherine, it is very certain, did not personally desire the dismemberment of Poland. Neither did she aim, at that time, at incorporating the whole of it in her own dominion. She had obtained the country by conquest, and preferred to keep it, as a whole, in complete subjection, so that it could never again give her any trouble, or resist her orders in future, whatever they might be. She would doubtless have had no scruples in setting aside her agreement with Prussia. She long hesitated on her course of policy. In the end she came to the conclusion that Russia was not then strong enough to digest so large a meal as the whole of Poland. There was grave discontent, throughout that country, with the conduct of the army of occupation. There were everywhere the smouldering embers of insurrection. A Prussian or an Austrian army, in support of a popular rising, might imperil her hold on it. She determined, therefore, to keep faith with Frederick William, and to admit him to a share in this big booty.

Meanwhile, the months which followed the subjection of Poland to Russia were occupied by Austria and Prussia in endless negotiations as to the indemnities they were respectively to aim at, for the expenses of the war with France, in which they were engaged as allies. There was this difference between their two positions. The King of Prussia had fully made up his mind as to what he wanted. He had set his heart on the acquisition of the province of Posen, and the cities of Thorn and Danzig, and as much more of Polish territory as he could squeeze out of Russia. The Emperor Francis, on the other hand, was perplexed as to what would best suit him, or what was most certain of acquisition, and, consequently, varied his demands from time to time. The rounding off of his dominions in the German Empire, by the acquisition of Bavaria, was what he most wished for. This he sometimes thought might be obtained by the exchange of Belgium for it, and at other times he hoped it might be seized and appropriated without any equivalent exchange. There were also the principalities of Anspach and Bayreuth, much desired by him. There was the possibility also of getting Alsace and Lorraine, or a slice of French Brabant, including Lille and Valenciennes, as an addition to Belgium, or the Venetian territory, which Austria had long coveted. Lastly, a share of Poland to balance those of Russia and Prussia in a new dismemberment and partition, would be very agreeable to him, either as a *pis aller* or as a superplus. The Emperor had difficulty in making up his mind between these possible accretions to his territory. No very certain agreement was come to between the two Courts. But it was well understood that Austria was to have an indemnity, either by exchange of Bavaria for Belgium, or elsewhere.

Subject to these arrangements as to future indemnities for the cost of the war, very certain as regards Prussia, very uncertain and undetermined as regards Austria—these two Powers invaded France in the summer of 1792. The entry was preceded by the notorious proclamation of the Duke of Brunswick, the Commander-in-Chief, dated July 20th, announcing on behalf of the Allies the destruction of the Revolution, and the restoration to Louis XVI of the powers he had been deprived of, and threatening dire vengeance on the population of Paris, or of any town or district in France, which should offer resistance. No one doubted the success of the invasion. Paris lay open to attack. The French army was disorganized by the emigration of the vast majority of its officers.

It is unnecessary to point out the failure of the invasion—how France rose in arms to resist it; how at Valmy it succeeded in arresting the Prussian army; how Brunswick was compelled to retreat; and how a counter-attack by the French on the Belgian province of the Emperor resulted at Jemappes, on November 9th, in the complete defeat of the Austrians, and their expulsion from Belgium; and how the French army was received with acclamation by the Belgian people. The campaign was a total failure as regards the Allies. The invasion of France led to the immediate deposition of Louis, and, ultimately, to the deaths of himself and the Queen by the guillotine.

On October 26th and 27th, after the retreat of the allied army from France, an important negotiation took place at Merle, in Luxemburg, at the headquarters of Frederick William, between representatives of Austria and Prussia, with reference to indemnities for the war. Haugwitz, on behalf of Prussia, displayed a map of Poland and pointed out a line of conquest traced on it by the King himself, and asserted that if immediate possession of the district, within the line, were not conceded to Prussia, her army on the Rhine would immediately retreat. Spielmann, on behalf of Austria, replied that Prussia would not obtain the consent of that Power to any acquisition in Poland, until the Emperor had obtained possession of Bavaria, and was assured of a superplus beyond that. Haugwitz, on his part, raised the objection that the circumstances of the time were little favourable for such an exchange within the Empire, but he added that the King of Prussia was ready to give his consent to it, if the Emperor insisted.* The King himself gave his personal assurance to that effect on the same day. In his interview with Frederick William, Spielmann threw out the suggestion that the three Powers might agree upon another dismemberment of Poland, and that Austria might take her share by way of pledge, and that if later an indemnity and a suitable superplus should elsewhere be found for her, she would then evacuate her share of Poland. This, he said, might be an inducement to the Poles to ratify to the other two Powers their shares in the dismemberment. This crafty plan commended itself to Frederick William. Spiel-

* Sorel, *L'Europe et la Révolution Française*, ii. p. 120.

mann, in reporting this to his Government, said: "If we refuse to the King of Prussia his just indemnity in Poland, he will withdraw from the coalition against France. Nothing will be easier, and the French will doubtless make a golden bridge for him to do so."

A fortnight after the meeting at Merle the battle of Jemappes was fought, on November 9th. It resulted in the complete subjection of Belgium by the French. It became clear to the Austrians that their scheme of the Bavarian exchange was very remote, if not impossible. The Emperor, therefore, notified to Prussia his intention to negotiate directly with Russia, and on December 23rd he made a demand on the Empress for a share of Poland. He claimed that the acquisitions of Prussia and himself should proceed *pari passu*, with the reservation that a sufficiency should be left of Poland to form a buffer State between the three Powers. In other words, Austria claimed a dismemberment of part of Poland, of the same kind as in 1772—that is, a partition, in equal lots, between the three Powers of the territory to be taken from Poland. Prussia also, about the same time, pressed its claim on Russia for a performance of the promise made to her. The Empress was willing to admit the claim of Prussia, but she rejected that of Austria.

Sybel quotes from the instructions given by the Empress Catherine about this time to Count Sievers, on his appointment as her Minister at Warsaw, which are very interesting as throwing light on the Russian policy.

"From the beginning," she said, "we have endeavoured to found our relations to Poland on an enduring basis, but the Poles, instead of meeting our advances with corresponding friendship, have only manifested the bitterest hatred; and then it came to our first partition in 1772, our consent to which, as all the initiated know, was only wrested from us by the force of circumstances." She added that ever since that she had manifested the same desire to protect the Poles, and had always met the same aversion; that after the revolution of May 3, 1791, she had summoned the Targowitzians, and procured from them and other friends and dependents the dominion over Poland. But she said that she had found them untrustworthy, selfish, and divided among themselves; that King Stanislaus was continually exciting his people and his army against Russia; that the Targowitzians complained that immediately on the withdrawal of the Russian troops a general revolution would break out; and that, to crown all, the poison of the French doctrines was spreading through the land. It was clear, under these circumstances, that no improvement was to be expected, and that she could only have in Poland a peaceful and harmless neighbour by reducing it to utter impotence. She then expressed her fears lest the King of Prussia should take possession of a Polish province without her concurrence, and enter into an understanding with the Polish patriots against Russia. She pointed out the danger that the King might conclude a peace with France, and that then her natural ally, the Emperor Francis, might fall into the greatest difficulties. In reality, however, resentment against Austria, which only eight months ago had proposed to her the union of Poland with Saxony, was the liveliest feeling in her heart, and what she feared was either the return of the Emperor to the same policy, or the concert of the two German Powers to effect a partition of Poland without Russian concurrence.

To avert these dangers, therefore, she resolved to close with Prussia as quickly as possible. This plan, she said, had undeniable advantages. "By adopting it we agree to an act whose whole result is to liberate from oppression all Russian lands and cities, peopled or founded by a cognate race, and confessing the same faith as ourselves. By uniting them with our Empire, we raise them to an equal pitch of glory and prosperity as our beloved subjects we hope enjoy." *

In this view she gave orders to her Ministers to negotiate with the Prussian Ambassador for a treaty of partition. The Empress, it was said, felt that it was necessary to lose no more time. She agreed to the acquisition by Prussia of the part of Poland so much desired by it, and the immediate seizure of it by the royal troops. She intended herself, she said, to incorporate a corresponding tract of country in the Ukraine.

This negotiation was kept secret from the Emperor Francis, who was clearly under the impression that Prussia had fully recognized the claim of Austria to an indemnity *pari passu* with her own, and would not come to

* Sybel, ii. pp. 387–8.

terms with Russia without admitting the Emperor to the bargain and providing satisfaction for him.

In spite of this, Prussia, behind the back of Austria, entered upon this secret negotiation with Russia. On January 23, 1793, a treaty was signed at St. Petersburg for the partition of rather less than half of the then existing territory of Poland. The share of Prussia under this treaty included the towns of Danzig and Thorn, which had been so long coveted by that Power, and the districts of Posen, Kalisch, and Plock, with an area of about 15,000 square miles and a population of over 1,000,000. Russia obtained the Palatinates of Kiev, Minsk, and Bracclaw and the greater part of Volhynia, with an area of about 90,000 square miles and a population of nearly 3,000,000—a proportion six times larger in extent, and nearly three times greater in population, than that reserved for Prussia. The areas thus annexed were to be incorporated as provinces of Russia and Prussia.

There remained a residue of Poland, about equal in area to that annexed by Russia. The treaty provided that it should retain a nominal independent existence, but was to be a close dependent of Russia and to be at best a vassal State. It was further provided in the treaty that the two Powers would endeavour to facilitate the exchange of Bavaria for Belgium, in the interest of Austria; but it was expressly said that this did not mean that force was to be used for the purpose. The King of Prussia also undertook to make common cause with the Emperor Francis in the war with France, and not to make peace until the object of the war was attained—namely, the destruction of the revolutionary Government, and the restoration of the Bourbons. It was provided that the treaty was to be kept secret until Prussia was put into actual possession of the district to be ceded to her, when the transaction would be presented to Austria as a *fait accompli*.

The treaty was a gross breach of good faith on the part of the King of Prussia against the Emperor, justifying all the suspicions which had been held by the latter. It amounted to this, that the King of Prussia succeeded in obtaining a considerable share of Poland, by way of indemnity for the expenses of a war in which the Emperor Francis was engaged as his ally, with the expectation and promise that he also would have a corresponding indemnity, without anything being secured to the latter, except a remote expectation of the Bavarian exchange, which Frederick William must have known would not be realized, and which, we may be very certain, he had no intention whatever of facilitating.

Already, before the formal signature of the treaty, and so soon as its terms were definitely decided on, Frederick William, with the approval of the Empress, gave orders to his army to march into Poland. For this purpose he recalled part of his army from the Rhine, and reinforced it by fresh levies in Silesia, bringing up the total force to 40,000, under General Möllendorf. He preceded the entry of his troops by a manifesto, dated January 6th, in which he announced to the sovereigns of Europe that the Jacobin intrigues in Poland compelled him, for the safety of his own country, to occupy a part of its frontier land. He claimed that he was rendering them a good service by crushing in Poland the principles of the French Revolution, and that he was giving new proofs of his affection and goodwill to the Poles. Being on the eve, he said, of another campaign in France, the two Imperial Courts concurred in the opinion that he ought, in good faith, to secure himself against attack by the seditious party in Poland. It was asserted at the time that emissaries had been sent to Poland from the Court of Berlin, with the object of forming Jacobin clubs, in order that their proceedings might furnish pretexts for the invasion and dismemberment. A similar device had been adopted by the Prussian Court in 1787 in Holland.*

On January 14th, General Möllendorf's army crossed the frontier of Poland in four columns from Silesia and East Prussia. They cut off and occupied the districts which, under the agreement with Catherine, were to be assigned to the King of Prussia. It was not, however, till the middle of February that rumours of the contents of the treaty reached the Emperor at Vienna, and not till March 25th that its actual terms were officially communicated to him. He then learned that his Allies were in full possession of their shares in the dismembered Poland, and that there was left to him, as his indemnity for the war, only the remote expectation of an exchange of Belgium for Bavaria, whenever the former should be reconquered from France.

* *Annual Register*, 1795, p. 21.

The announcement caused the greatest indignation at Vienna. The duplicity of Prussia in making this secret treaty with Russia, behind the back of Austria, and thus securing a large share of the dismembered Poland, without any certain compensation for Austria, was bitterly resented. Cobenzl, who had so recently superseded Kaunitz as chief Minister of the Emperor, and Spielmann, who was so largely responsible for the negotiations with Prussia, were at once dismissed. Cobenzl was succeeded by Baron Thugut, who had risen from the ranks by his great ability and industry, but who was wholly without principles or scruples.

Thugut held the opinion that any aggrandizement of Prussia would be a very grave misfortune to Austria. This was the key to his policy for the next few years, during the revolutionary period. On April 19th, he instructed the Austrian Ambassador at St. Petersburg to inform the Empress that his master, the Emperor Francis, desired to renew the intimate relations which had been arrived at between the two Courts in 1781. He was to entreat the Empress to defer the final settling of the claims of Prussia in Poland. He was to ask what compensation was intended for

Austria, and to point out that the scheme of the Bavarian exchange was fraught with great difficulty. In any case, it could not be considered as an equivalent for the acquisitions of Russia and Prussia in Poland, for though it would result in rounding off the Emperor's possessions in Germany, it would mean on the balance an actual diminution of territory. Compensation, therefore, would be due to Austria equivalent to the acquisitions of Russia and Prussia in Poland.

"It is with regret," he added, "that the Emperor will decide to seek in Poland, after the example of these two Courts, an acquisition which, by right and justice, is due to him, but this must be inevitable in default of some other scheme of indemnity." He protested also against the excessive extent of the area of Poland allotted to Prussia. The Emperor Francis, at the same time, wrote in his own hand to Catherine. "I insist persistently," he said, "in demanding for Austria an absolute equality of acquisition and other advantages with Russia and Prussia." Catherine, in reply, contented herself with saying that the matter as regards the share of Prussia in Poland was already settled, and could not be reopened. She admitted that this was larger than that Power was entitled to. She held out no hopes of a similar concession to Austria.

The discussion was renewed at St. Petersburg in July. The Austrian Ambassador was instructed to demand the cession of the Polish district of Cracow. The following interesting conversation took place between the Russian Minister, Markoff, and Cobenzl, the Austrian Ambassador. The former suggested that French Flanders, Alsace, Lorraine, Bavaria, and even Turkey offered greater advantages to Austria than Poland.

"We only ask for a share of Poland," was the reply of the Ambassador, "as a *pis aller*. We would prefer a province conquered from France, but the conquest is not achieved, and in spite of all our efforts, and our firm resolution to continue the war, it is possible that we may not succeed. The Elector Palatine of Bavaria and his heir refuse to barter their patrimony against Belgium, and the King of Prussia, in an underhand way, incites them to resist. In order to despoil Turkey there must be another war. Where, then, can we get an equivalent except in Poland?"

"That miserable kingdom in such case would be entirely destroyed," said the Russian.

"What does that matter," was the reply, "in comparison with the danger that will arise to Austria, if she has not an equivalent to that obtained by Prussia?"*

The discussion led to no immediate result.

Meanwhile the Prussian army, under General Möllendorf, took possession of the districts in Poland assigned to his country. They met with no opposition, except on the part of the German town of Danzig. They simply took the place of Russian troops who evacuated these districts. The Confederates of Targowitz had some remnant of patriotism, which induced them to object to the Prussian invasion. They were under the impression that the Empress Catherine intended to respect the integrity of their country, and was acting in good faith, when she called them into existence as a rival to the Diet of Warsaw. They issued a protest against the invasion by the Prussians, and finally declared that they would not submit to any further dismemberment of their country. They also appealed to the Empress against the proceedings of Prussia. They protested that they were bound by their oaths, as members of the Diet, to maintain

* Sorel, iii. p. 352.

the integrity of their country. The Empress replied that if they attempted to resist the Prussians, they would have to deal with the Russian troops. This sufficed to shut the mouths of the Targowitzians.

King Stanislaus, on April 23rd, wrote to Catherine expressing a wish to abdicate his throne. "My duty," he said, "forbids me to take any part in measures which will bring disaster on Poland." Catherine cynically replied that she had not made him King of Poland in order that he might surrender the throne, at the very moment when he could best serve the interests of Russia by remaining there. It was necessary for her that there should be a King of Poland in order to sanction the treaty which would dismember his country. Stanislaus received an order from her to remain in her employment until there was no longer a Poland. The assigned districts made no further resistance to the Prussian and Russian invaders.

Count Sievers, the new Ambassador, as he was called, of the Empress at Warsaw, was one of those supple, dexterous, plausible, insinuating, and unscrupulous men, whom Russia, at that time, had in her employment, ready to oil the wheels of some new annexation of territory. It was the wish of the Empress to obtain from the Diet of Poland a treaty, ceding to Russia and Prussia the parts of their country, which she had decided to wrest from them. It was the task of Sievers to effect this object, peacefully, as far as possible, but by threats of force and by bribery if necessary.

The "generality," set up by the Targowitzians, had already been removed to Grodno, so as to be more under the influence of Russia. Most of its members were in the pay of the Russian Government. It was directed by Sievers to issue writs for the election of a new Diet. Only those parts of the country, which were to be left in nominal independence, and which were not to be annexed as provinces by Russia or Prussia, were called upon to elect nuncios. The election took place under the skilful management of Sievers. General Igelström, who commanded the Russian troops in Poland, received the following order with regard to the election: "The General will carry on the election of deputies to the Diet by means of Russian Staff officers, and detachments of troops, who will drive out all those who are not favourable to the matter in hand, and only admit compliant persons." This rule was strictly followed. Electors were forbidden to vote for members of the previous Diet who had supported the Constitution of 1791. Bribery also was largely resorted to. Sievers sent word to St. Petersburg that, in his opinion, a Diet had never gone cheaper, that he could get forty votes for 2,000 ducats.

The Diet did not meet till June 17, 1793. Sievers then presented to it for approval a treaty with Russia, ceding the parts of Poland, which the Empress had decided to incorporate as a Russian province. As regards that part of Poland which was still to be allowed to retain an appearance of nominal but dependent existence, Russia promised to guarantee for the future its Constitution, not the reformed one of 1791, but its anarchical predecessor. The Diet was to be prohibited making any change in this, without the consent of the Russian Government. The treaty further guaranteed full religious freedom, and encouragement to Polish commerce. In spite of the electoral manipulation of Sievers, there were still a few members elected, who could not be relied on to carry out his orders. The Diet was surrounded and overawed by Russian troops.

Even under these conditions, the Diet made some show of resistance, and delayed, as long as possible, giving their sanction to the treaty, which proposed to dismember their country. A minority made stubborn resistance. On July 1st, Sievers found himself compelled to overcome this opposition by arresting and deporting to Siberia seven leaders of the patriotic party, and by directing the confiscation of the property of others. In spite of these strong measures, the Diet still delayed coming to a conclusion. On July 16th, Sievers informed them that he would consider any further delay as a declaration of war, and that he would proceed to military measures, of the most extreme kind, against those of the Assembly who persisted in opposing the general wish of the nation. There were even then eloquent protests in the Diet.

"They want to send us to Siberia!" exclaimed one of the most influential of the patriots. "Let them do so, the threat has no terrors for us"; and addressing the King, who was present, he added: "You, Sire, conduct us, if it must be so, into Siberia. Let us go from here, where we are menaced, into those melancholy wastes. There, at least, our virtues will cover with confusion those who conspire our ruin." (Here the deputies cried unanimously, "Let us go to Siberia!") "We are your children and will follow you with the enthusiasm of grateful love; and the measure of your suffering shall be exceeded by our earnest veneration." Stanislaus, however, had no wish or intention to make a martyr of himself, by leading them to Siberia. He pointed out to the Assembly that resistance was no longer possible. The majority of the Diet, thinking that its honour was sufficiently saved by the force already used against many of its members, and threatened against them all, gave way, and on July 25th the Diet, by a vote of 61 to 23, ratified the treaty, ceding to Russia the territory which the Empress had signified her intention to incorporate as a province. It amounted to about two-fifths of the kingdom of Poland reduced by the partition of 1772. Stanislaus added his signature to the treaty the same day.

Sievers, having settled the matter to his satisfaction, so far as Russia was concerned, informed the Diet that the Empress further insisted on their ratifying another treaty with Prussia, ceding to that Power a further large part of Poland which she had assigned to it. This was more than the Diet, though elected by means of military force and bribery of Russia, could stomach. They did their utmost to resist. On September 23rd the Diet was again surrounded by Russian troops. Four of the most distinguished of the patriots were arrested and deported, as a menace to the others. The Diet demanded the liberation of the four members, declaring that they were deprived by violence of the freedom of deliberation. This was refused. The Russian General in command of the troops then enjoined them insolently, with threats and admonitions, to sign the treaty required of them. The Assembly remained inactive and silent for several hours. At three o'clock in the morning the deputy for Cracow moved that the Diet should draw up a formal protest against the violation of their liberties by the Russian Ambassador, and that their dissent should be marked by profound silence. This course was adopted. The treaty was again presented to them. The order of the Empress was read by Sievers, directing them, without delay, to sanction the terms agreed upon with Prussia. There was a dead silence throughout the hall. The President thereupon declared that the silence of the deputies meant their consent, and that the Prussian treaty was *ipso facto* sanctioned.

A formal protest was then signed by the King and the Diet against the violent actions of the two Courts of Russia and Prussia. "I, the King of Poland," it ran, "enfeebled by age, and sinking under the accumulated weight of so many misfortunes, and we members of the Diet, hereby declare that, being unable, even by the sacrifice of our lives, to relieve our country from the yoke of its oppressors, consign it to posterity, trusting that means may be found, at some happier period, to rescue it from oppression and slavery; such means, unfortunately, are not in our power, and other countries abandon us to our fate."

After the dismemberment of Poland effected by these two treaties, ratified by the Diet under compulsion, there remained about two-fifths of the country still undealt with. The disposition and future status of this was provided for by another treaty with Russia, which was ratified by the Polish Diet at the dictation of Sievers on October 5, 1793.

By this treaty the absolute dependence of

this residue on Russia was amply secured. It was to retain a nominal existence, and was not to be incorporated as a Russian province, but it was to be completely subject to the will of the Russian Government. The two States were mutually to aid one another in any future war, and the command of their troops was to fall to the Power which furnished the greater number—that is, Russia. Russia was further authorized at all times to send its troops into Poland, and to have them maintained there. Poland was never to make any change in its Constitution, without the consent of Russia. Sievers, in explaining the new arrangement to his mistress, the Empress, wrote: "With respect to the present King, the hapless Stanislaus, we must hold the rod over him. . . . His task must be assigned to him. He will receive a *major domo*, under the title of a Russian Ambassador, invested with more power than ever the Viceroy of Ireland possessed, or even your own Governor-General of Novgorod. The future King will be chosen by your Majesty."* The relation to Russia, therefore, of what remained of Poland was that of complete and absolute subjection. When a deputy of the

* Sybel, iii. p. 154.

Polish Diet ventured to make the remark that the treaty of alliance was, in fact, a treaty of subjection he met with the reply that resistance to it would only increase the evil.

The sham Diet of Targowitz was dissolved by order of the Empress shortly after the partition. The Diet at Grodno, after its act of submission to Russia, continued its session for four weeks, and was finally dissolved on November 23rd. During this time it showed great activity. It annulled all the decrees of the confederated Diet of Targowitz.

Sievers, the astute agent of the Empress, having accomplished his task of carrying through this amazing transaction, was recalled. It was thought by his employers, at St. Petersburg, that he was too conciliatory for the work of governing Poland. His functions were conferred on General Igelström, the General in command of the Russian forces in Poland, who exercised his powers with insolent brutality. Poland was practically placed under the military despotism of Russia. Stanislaus became a subordinate agent of the Russian Government.

CHAPTER VIII

HOW POLAND SAVED FRANCE

THERE remained of the Kingdom of Poland, as an abject dependency of Russia, after the second partition in 1793, a territory of about two-fifths of its original extent. This consisted of what was, and still is known as Great Poland, the whole of Lithuania, and parts of Galicia and Podolia. This residuum of a great kingdom was to be divided up by the three neighbouring Powers, within the next two years, after a desperate but futile attempt of the Poles to regain their independence. To understand what took place —how Russia, with the aid of Prussia, succeeded in putting down this outbreak of the Poles, and how Austria, after its complete discomfiture by Prussia, in the second partition of Poland, was able to assert herself and to obtain a full share in the third partition, and also to fathom the perfidies of Austria and Prussia to one another, and to Poland, and to explain how these two Powers were drawn off the scent of their attack on France by the lure of plunder in Poland—it is necessary to revert to the course of events in their campaign of 1793.

The previous year's campaign of 1792 had not realized the confident expectations of Austria and Prussia. Instead of resulting in the defeat of the French, the march to Paris of the Allied army, and the overthrow of the Revolution, it had exactly the opposite result. The Allies were defeated, and were compelled to retreat across the frontier. The French occupied and made themselves masters of Belgium, and threatened Holland. It was under these circumstances that, early in 1793, the two German Powers had to determine whether to embark on another campaign against France.

The Emperor Francis would not as yet recognize defeat. He was in favour of another campaign, in the hope of recovering his lost province. He still counted on putting an end to the Revolution in France. The King of Prussia, on the other hand, was not interested in reinstating the Emperor in his Belgian province. But he had entered into an agreement with the Empress Catherine to continue the war with France, until its objects were achieved—that is, till the Revolution was put down; and as this was the condition on which he was to be permitted to share in the dismemberment and plunder of Poland, and as it was still possible that the Empress might withdraw from her engagement, if he made peace with France, he decided to continue the war as the ally, however unwilling, of the Emperor. It will be seen, however, that he was not disposed to make any vigorous efforts for success, and that his interests were much more engaged in Poland than in Belgium.

Another event, which mainly contributed to the renewal of the war, was the entry of Great Britain into the field, and its decision to join with the two German Powers in their coalition against France. Mr. Pitt, the powerful Minister of George III, had thus far persistently opposed any measures which would involve England in the war. The revolutionary proceedings of the National Assembly, and the personal danger of Louis XVI and his family, did not draw him from this policy of neutrality. Remembering the part taken by France, in the still recent war between England and its colonies, his Government probably were not sorry to see France weakened by internal strife, and by war with the two German Powers. George III also had no special sympathy for his brother-monarch. He made no serious effort to save Louis even from the extreme penalty of death. Pitt maintained, therefore, the most correct attitude of neutrality during the campaign of 1792.

The unexpected defeat, however, of the invading German army at Valmy, and its retreat across the frontier, the successful counter-attack of the French on Belgium, and the threatened attack on Holland, drew the British Government at last from its reserve. On November 13, 1792, Pitt decided to open correspondence with the two German Powers, with a view to common action against France. Dispatches to this effect were sent by Lord Grenville to the British Ambassadors at Vienna and Berlin. They were of a cautious character, not committing the Government to any positive action, but they were not the less significant of the intention of the British Government as against France, and, if made public, would undoubtedly have been regarded by the Convention at Paris as menace of hostility.

"Unforeseen events," it was said in the

letter to Sir Morton Eden at Berlin, "and more particularly the success of the French army in Flanders, have brought forward considerations in which the common interests of England and Prussia are deeply concerned. There are grave reasons to fear for the security and tranquillity of the United Provinces [Holland]; and the British Government now asks for confidential communications from the Court of Berlin." * A similar letter was sent to Ewart at Vienna.

It was not till two months later, on January 12, 1793, that the Governments of Austria and Prussia replied to these overtures by sending their representatives in London to interview Grenville at the Foreign Office. The two Ministers explained that the long delay in replying to Grenville's dispatch of November 13th was due to their Governments being engaged in considering a project for indemnifying themselves for the expenses of the war against France. A scheme had now been arranged between them by which Prussia was to get, by way of indemnity, an arrondissement on the side of Poland, and in return was to withdraw opposition to the exchange by Austria

* Grenville to Eden, November 13, 1792. Record Office.

of the Low Countries and Bavaria. Grenville very properly told them that "the King [George III] would never be a party to any concert or plan one part of which was the giving of compensation for the expenses of the war from a neutral and unoffending nation; that the King was bound by no engagement of any sort with Poland, but that neither would his Majesty's sentiments suffer him to participate in measures directed to such an object, nor could he hope for the concurrence and support of his people in such a system. . . . If France persisted in a war of mere aggrandizement, her opponents might justly expect some compensation; but the compensation, however arranged, could be looked for only from conquests made from France, and not from the invasion of the territory of another country." *

A few days later Eden wrote from Berlin stating the determination of the King of Prussia no longer to act as a principal in the war, if the indemnification in Poland was refused to him. He added that on asking the Prussian Minister if Russia had preferred any claim of the same kind, the reply was that nothing had

* Grenville to Eden, January 12, 1793. Record Office.

as yet been settled, but that Russia had views of aggrandizement on the side of Poland, that Austria also must look for indemnification in the same direction, as it was not likely that the projected exchange of Bavaria could be carried out.*

In the meantime, since the overtures of November 13th of the previous year, most important events had occurred which strengthened the determination of the British Government to take part in the war. On November 16th the Convention at Paris issued the decree throwing open to all the world the navigation of the River Scheldt. This was held by the British Government to be a grave breach of the rights of Holland, guaranteed to it by the Treaty of Westphalia and later treaties, to which France had been a party, and in respect of which England, under the treaty with Holland of 1788, guaranteeing its integrity, was bound to take up the cause of the Dutch as against France.

On November 19th, another decree was issued by the Convention, offering the aid of France to any peoples in arms against their Governments. The French army in Belgium had by

* Eden to Grenville, January 19, 1793. Record Office.

this time made itself completely master of that country, and was threatening invasion of Holland. On January 21, 1793, the execution of Louis XVI took place, an act which aroused a deep feeling of indignation throughout Europe, and nowhere more so than in England. The war party there received an immense impetus, and the maintenance of peace with France became hopeless. The British Government decided on the violent measure of directing the expulsion from the country of Chauvelin, the emissary of France, who had been in negotiation with them, and also on prohibiting the export of corn to that country. These acts were construed by the French Convention as the deliberate intention of the British Government to join the coalition against them, and on February 1st they made a formal declaration of war against England.

On February 5, 1793, before this declaration was known in England, Grenville wrote to Eden at Berlin informing him that the King desired to enter into a formal engagement with the King of Prussia and the Emperor of Austria, for the prosecution of war with France. With respect to the claims made by the representatives of these two Powers, on January 13th, for indemnification for the expenses of the war, Grenville, in his dispatch, said:—

"Of that part of the plan which relates to Poland, I have already stated in the most unequivocal terms the King's disapproval of that project, against which you have made such frequent, though ineffectual, representations. It is, however, of a nature entirely unconnected with the settlement of the affairs of France, and though his Majesty never can consider it but with disapprobation and regret, he has no intent to oppose himself to its execution by any measures on his part. . . . The Austrian part of the plan appears in every point of view considerably less objectionable, though certainly attended with great difficulty. But the execution of such, if it can be carried into effect, depends on obliging the French to withdraw from the Belgian provinces." *

Grenville, when he wrote in these terms, knew that in view of the difficulties of effecting the Bavarian exchange, Austria had also preferred a claim for a share in the dismemberment of Poland, and that Russia, to whom he made similar overtures at the same

* Grenville to Eden, February 5, 1793. Record Office.

time, was also determined on aggrandizement in the same direction.

It will be observed that Grenville's language, on this occasion, was very different from that used in his interview with the representatives of Austria and Prussia, on January 13th. He was now virtually agreeing, on the part of the British Government, to adopt the very course which he had then repudiated. Subject to a mild and ineffectual protest, he was offering to make England "a party to a concert, one part of which was the giving of compensation for the expenses of the war from a neutral and unoffending nation"—Poland. It is difficult, under these circumstances, to acquit Pitt and his Government of some share of responsibility for the undoing, and subsequent partition of Poland.

None of these dispatches were laid before the British Parliament, or were alluded to in the explanation made by Pitt and other Ministers, when asking for means to carry on the war, in concert with Austria and Prussia. The war was justified and defended, mainly on the ground of the breach by France of its treaty obligations to Holland, by the opening of the navigation of the River Scheldt. It is on this ground also that it has been justified by the greater number of historians who have written on the revolutionary period.

"It was impossible for Pitt," has said one of the latest and most distinguished of them, Lord Rosebery, in his *Life of Pitt*, "to pass by his own treaty of 1788, with respect to the Scheldt, without a violation of good faith so signal as to be remarkable even in the time of the second partition of Poland. But on wider grounds the danger to Europe was more universal. To allow that the French Government were in possession of a law of nature which superseded treaty obligations, and the copyright and application of which vested exclusively with them, was to annihilate the whole European system." *

In the earlier debates on the war in Parliament, in the year 1793, there was no allusion to Poland. The objections raised to the war by Charles Fox, in his many speeches, were mainly that the Dutch Government had not called upon England to support them in opposing the action of the French, in the matter of the Scheldt, and that there was no obligation on the part of England to make it a *casus belli*,

* Rosebery's *Life of Pitt*, p. 125.

unless called upon to do so by the Dutch. When challenged on this point by Fox in the House of Commons, Pitt was obliged to admit that the Government of Holland had made no demand on England to support them by war, in resisting the opening of the river.

"England," said Fox on February 19, 1793, "is bound, by virtue of the treaty of 1788, to protect the Dutch, if they call upon us to do so, but neither by honour nor by treaty till then. . . . We are bound to save Holland from war, or by war, if called upon. But to force the Dutch into war, at so much peril to them, is not to fulfil, but to abuse the treaty."

Later in the year, when the intentions of Russia and Prussia to dismember Poland became known, Fox dealt with the subject, in an attack on the war, in the following language:—

"As to the general danger to Europe, England has been shamefully inattentive; it has seen the partition of Poland with marked indifference. . . . Did not the seizure and spoil of Poland lead to the aggrandizement of the Powers by whom it was perpetrated? Was it not a greater and more contemptuous violation of the laws of nations than the French had been guilty of? Had we opposed it? If Ministers had any such remonstrances to show they would produce them in due time, and then the House would judge them, but while none were produced or even mentioned he must presume that none had been made." *

Later again Fox moved a series of resolutions against the war, in one of which he dealt with the case of Poland in the following terms:—

" Some of the present Powers engaged in the confederacy against France have openly avowed and successfully executed plans of conquest, not less formidable to the general liberties of Europe. This rapacity and faithless dismemberment of the unhappy kingdom of Poland, without having produced, so far as it appears, any remonstrance from his Majesty's Ministers, has excited indignation at so daring an outrage on the rights of independent nations, and the keenest solicitude to rescue the honour of the British Government from the suspicion of having concurred or acquiesced in measures so odious in their principles, and so dangerous in the example, to the peace and happiness of mankind." †

This was one of a series of resolutions in favour of bringing the war to an end proposed in June 1793, when Holland and Belgium had been completely evacuated by the French. In the course of his speech in support of them, Fox said: "Let us ask ourselves, with all the indignation we naturally entertain against

* *Parliamentary History*, February 12, 1792.

† Ibid., June 17, 1793.

the conduct of France, whether the conduct of the Courts of Berlin and St. Petersburg in their invasion and partition of Poland is not equal in infamy to that of France."

Fox's language would probably have been far stronger, and might possibly have had greater effect on the House of Commons, if it had been known that the King of Prussia had only consented to prolong the war against France, upon the express understanding that he was to receive indemnity for his expenses, in a definite assignment of a conquered and dismembered Poland.

Pitt, in his reply, avoided any mention of the subject of Poland. He defined in clear and concise language the case of England in the war, viz :—

1. That France had broken a treaty with the allies of England which she was bound to support.

2. That she had engaged in schemes of ambition and aggrandizement inconsistent with the general security of Europe.

3. That she had entertained principles hostile to all Governments, and more particularly to that of England.

The first two of these propositions applied

with even more force to the action of Russia, Prussia, and Austria, and especially of Prussia, in regard to the broken treaty with Poland of 1791. Burke, who spoke in defence of the Government in the course of the debate, said, in reference to Poland:—

> "Whatever were his sentiments with regard to Poland, he should think it wise to hold his tongue, for was it possible for Great Britain to go to war with Austria, Russia, and Prussia with no ally but France? And what Government was there in France with which we could form an alliance? . . . The situation of France rendered any such alliance impracticable; for, with respect to England, it might be considered as a country in the moon. . . . The partition of Poland might possibly be made so as not to destroy, or even to affect, in any degree, the balance of power in Europe. The King of Prussia had taken Danzig, and he (Mr. Burke) was sorry for it, but had he taken the life or the property of any individual?"

The House of Commons rejected the resolution of Fox by a majority of 187 to 47.

Meanwhile, the campaign of 1793 had commenced. The British Government, early in March, sent three battalions of Guards to Holland. The question of indemnity for the expenses of the war now became a very urgent one. Pitt, who at one time had been not unwilling to consent to the Bavarian exchange, now reverted to his original opposition to it. The Emperor Francis was partially appeased by a proposal, first suggested by Sir Morton Eden, that compensation should be found for him by a slice of France, on the frontier of Belgium, including the important fortresses of Lille and Valenciennes.* This would strengthen the frontier of Belgium against France, and might induce the Bavarian Elector to agree to the exchange.

It was obvious that in this general scheme of indemnities England could not be left in the lurch. On the suggestion, it was said, of the Duke of Buckingham, the brother of Grenville, it was decided by the Government to claim the port of Dunkirk at the close of the war.† This, it was said, would be a useful *point d'appui* for England, in the future, for the better protection of British interests in Belgium and Holland, and its occupation would prevent its being a nest for privateers, as it had been in past wars. The acquisition by Austria of French Flanders would make it more easy for England to hold Dunkirk. The proposal was defended historic-

* Fortescue's *History of the British Army*, vol. vi. p. 83.
† Ibid. p. 84.

ally, on the ground that it had been more than once in olden times in possession of the British Crown, that Cromwell, in 1658, had acquired possession of it, and that it had been sold to France, in 1662, by Charles II in order to fill his empty pockets. It was further proposed that England should recoup herself for war expenses by the capture of some, if not all, of the French colonies.

There was a good deal of counting chickens before they were hatched in all these negotiations as to indemnities for the expenses of the war. It will be seen that the decision arrived at had a disastrous effect on the strategy of the war. The three Powers engaged in it against France, jealous of one another, and thinking mainly of what each would gain in territory, diverted their armies from the main object, the defeat of France, and lost whatever prospect there was of marching to Paris and putting an end to the Revolution. The war, avowedly begun by England for the purpose of vindicating international law, and the faith of treaties, and as regards the other two Powers for preventing the spread of the Revolution, became one in which the three Powers were each of them to acquire territory or colonies, at the expense of France, and of unoffending Poland.

For a time, however, everything went well with the Allies. Even before the main army of England arrived at the seat of war in Flanders, the French had failed in their attempt, early in the year, to invade Holland. Their army, under General Dumouriez, which had crossed the frontier from Belgium, and had taken Breda, was forced by the Dutch, assisted by the British Guards, to retreat. This was followed up by the Austrians, and on March 18, 1793, Dumouriez met with a signal defeat by the Prince of Coburg, at Neerwinden. This great battle had the effect of freeing the whole of Belgium from the French. Their high-handed proceedings, the utter want of discipline, and the disorders and maraudings of their army had completely alienated the Belgians, who only six months previously had received them with enthusiasm. Later Dumouriez, who had been very badly treated by the Convention at Paris, and who was a Royalist at heart, offered to come to terms with Coburg, and to lead his army against the Convention at Paris. When he found that the army would not follow him, he deserted the French army, and with a few officers and men went over to the Austrians, and thus brought his career to an inglorious end.

The main British Army, which consisted of about 20,000 men, had arrived too late to take part in the battle of Neerwinden. It was now to be used in an offensive campaign against France. It was quite inadequate in numbers and equipment for this purpose. Its commander, the Duke of York, a son of George III, a young man of many good parts and excellent intentions, and with the courage of his race, was quite incompetent to undertake a great campaign. He had the unfortunate habit of losing his presence of mind when any serious emergency occurred. The King had insisted on his employment. The Ministers, greatly doubting whether they were justified in acceding, thought that the Duke's royal rank would facilitate co-operation in the Allied armies, when the Emperor of Austria and the King of Prussia were present in the field. Mr. Dundas (later Lord Melville), the most incompetent administrator who ever, in any country, filled the post of War Minister, reconciled himself to the appointment of the Duke, by the observation that "the capture of Dunkirk by a Prince of the Blood would give *éclat* to the opening of the campaign."

A conference took place at Antwerp, on April 8th, of the generals and diplomatic agents of the Allied forces for the purpose of determining on the coming campaign against France. It is worth while to describe the scene which took place there, for it indicates clearly the spirit in which the Allies prepared to conduct it. The Prince of Coburg had issued a manifesto, in which he disclaimed, on behalf of the Allies, any intention to deprive France of any territory. The Conference was presided over by the Duke of York. Coburg, on behalf of the Austrians, assuming that the object of the war was the destruction of the Revolution in France, and the restoration of its monarchy, laid down the proposition, in conformity with his manifesto, that there should be a self-denying ordinance, to the effect that no territorial conquests should be made by the Allies.

Count Starhenberg, the Austrian envoy, in his report to his Government at Vienna, says:—

"This proposal of Coburg sounded the tocsin of indignation to all the other members of the conference. Lord Auckland, the British representative, saw in it the sign of treachery on the part of Austria, and his anger was so great that he was on the point of withdrawing. The Duke of York was also hot with rage, and considered himself as tricked by Coburg. The Prince of Nassau and his sons followed on the same impulse as their allies. Coburg, frightened by the storm he had roused, endeavoured to allay it.

"'Being in no way versed in the mysteries of politics,' he said, 'I had thought till now that the object of the Powers in coalition was to re-establish the monarchy in France and order and peace in Europe. . . . I find that I am mistaken. I see that every one is thinking only of himself, and has much less in view the general interest than that of his own country only.' . . . Lord Auckland made it clearly understood that the restoration of order did not interest him at all, and announced, with much vivacity, that the wish of England was to reduce France to a veritable political nullity. . . . 'Each of the Powers in coalition,' he added, 'should seek to make conquests and keep them when made.' Then, addressing Coburg, he said: 'Take all the frontier fortresses of France on your side and obtain a good barrier for Belgium. As to England, I will frankly say she wishes to make conquests and she will keep them. She desires Dunkirk and intends also to find her compensation in the colonies of France.' The Dutch representative made a claim also for compensation on behalf of Holland. The Conference separated in a state of irritation against Coburg." *

Coburg was compelled to withdraw his manifesto and to issue a new one, in which

* Sorel, *L'Histoire de la Révolution*, vol. iii. p. 366. He gives as authority for this the reports of Starhenberg to Thugut, and of Coburg to the Emperor Francis of April 12, 1793.

there was no disclaimer of territorial acquisition, at the cost of France. Though there was nothing in the report of Starhenberg about Poland, or about the Bavarian exchange, it was no doubt well understood by members of the Conference that Prussia would take its indemnity out of the former. As regards Bavaria, though the British Government strongly objected to the scheme of exchange, the Austrian Emperor had not given it up, for about this time Thugut sent an emissary to London again to press this scheme on the British Government. Austria, he said, would do its best to increase the territory of Belgium by conquest from France of her border fortresses. He evidently thought that this addition to Belgium, strengthening it as against France, would make his scheme more palatable to England. He added that unless England consented to the exchange of Bavaria, he would be obliged to claim a share of Poland. At the same time, Thugut, with his accustomed duplicity, informed the Empress Catherine, who had agreed to guarantee the Bavarian exchange if Austria would agree to the partition treaty, that the Emperor renounced the scheme of exchange, and looked for his indemnity both in France and Poland.

Sir Morton Eden also informed the Prussian Government that England would not agree to the scheme of exchange. The King of Prussia replied to this that if Austria thwarted his designs on Poland, he would withdraw his troops from France, except the 20,000 which, as member of the Empire, he was bound to maintain there as his contingent to the Imperial army.

The result of the machinations of the three Powers, each thinking of his own interests only, and especially of the duplicity of Austria, under the advice of Thugut, was soon apparent in the campaign against France. The scheme of the Bavarian exchange was bitterly resented, if not by the aged Elector Palatine of Bavaria, by his family and expectant heir. They raised difficulties to the passage of the Austrian troops through Bavarian territory to the Rhine, and refused to allow Mannheim to be used as a *place d'armes* for the Allies. The Emperor of Austria thereupon detained a large part of his reserves from going to Flanders, in the hope that he might find an opportunity and excuse for taking forcible possession of Bavaria. This gave excuse for the retention at home of the Bavarian contingent to the Imperial army, in order to watch the Austrians. The Prussians also, more intent on Poland, where they were to have a share of the booty, than on Flanders and France, where they were to have no territorial aggrandizement, reduced their army on the Rhine by sending a large part of it to Poland. It will be seen also that the British Government, instead of concentrating all its available force on Flanders for the defeat of the French armies, and the invasion of France, frittered away the greater part of it on expeditions to various parts of the world, to Toulon and Corsica, and to St. Domingo and other West Indian Islands belonging to France, which it hoped to annex by way of indemnity. The very reduced force of British troops which remained available, increased by Hanoverians and Hessians, in British pay, instead of being concentrated with the Austrians for the main purposes of the campaign, was diverted to Dunkirk, with the intention of securing this as part of the British indemnity for the war. Thus it was that the success of the great combination of the Allied forces was compromised, even before the campaign of 1793 was commenced. The hope of gaining indemnity for the war by the dismemberment of Poland was the main cause of this great failure.

The immediate result, however, of the Conference at Antwerp of the generals and diplomatic agents of the Allied armies was a project for the campaign about to commence. The armies of Austria, England, and Holland, instead of invading France in combination with the Prussian and Imperial armies on the Rhine, masking the frontier fortresses, and marching to Paris, as they might well have done, in view of the demoralization of the French army, were to be employed in besieging and reducing these strongholds. The Austrians and British were to capture Condé and Valenciennes. After that the British army was to to be diverted to Dunkirk, while the Austrians were to besiege Quesnoy. Meanwhile the Prussians, under the Duke of Brunswick, were to capture Mainz and thence to march westwards. After the reduction of these fortresses the three armies were to combine for the invasion of France.

For a time this scheme appeared to offer hopes of success. After much delay Condé was captured on July 10th and Valenciennes on the 28th, while Mainz fell to the Prussians on the 22nd. The Austrian and British armies then, most unwisely, separated. The Duke of York's army marched westward to the sea, and appeared before Dunkirk, which it was unable to invest. The Convention, under the inspiration of Carnot, who then first showed his great organizing power and his military genius, sent an army, under General Houchard, to relieve Dunkirk. He succeeded in this, and defeated and drove back the Duke with great loss. If he had followed up this victory, he might have overwhelmed the British force. For the neglect of this he was sent to the guillotine by the Convention. The Duke, escaping from Houchard, found his way eastward again, and joined with Coburg, who had taken Quesnoy, and together they invested Maubeuge.

The Convention in Paris, meanwhile, had found time to make a *levée en masse.* Their army in the North of France, reinforced, and, under the command of Jourdan, used with an entire disregard of the loss of life, attacked the combined army in front of Maubeuge, and compelled it to withdraw from the siege. After this the two armies went into winter quarters, at the end of October. The Prussian army, having taken Mainz, made no further advance.

Farther east, the Imperial forces, under Wurmser, attacked the French army in Alsace, and drove it from the lines of Wissenberg on October 15th. If supported, even then, by the Prussian army in front of Mainz, much might still have been effected. But the Prussians had no wish to facilitate Austrian projects for the conquest of Alsace, and refused or neglected to move. The King of Prussia left this army and betook himself to Posen, in order to take part in the dismemberment of Poland. The campaign of 1793 came to an end with little result, except the capture of three or four frontier fortresses.

Throughout the early part of this year the prospects of a successful invasion of France for the purpose of putting down the Revolution were exceedingly favourable, if the Allied Powers had been really zealous for the purpose, and had acted in full accord. France was torn by internal dissension. The Royalist party was still very strong. Lyons, Marseilles, and Toulon were in its hands. The National army was disorganized. But the want of union and the jealousies and the greed of territory of the Great Powers, and especially of Austria and Prussia, ruined their cause.

The delay in the main attack, and the frittering away of their forces on the capture of fortresses, gave time to France to organize a national defence. The Committee of Public Safety was reorganized by the addition of Carnot, Prieur, and Lindet. Nothing in history has been more surprising than the efforts of these three strong and determined men for saving France from her invaders.

No one who surveys carefully the whole field of European politics, and the military movements of this time, can doubt that Poland was the salvation of France. It was the apple of discord between Austria and Prussia. It distracted the attention of both these nations from the main objective of their campaign against France. It was the cause of greed for territory being substituted for hostility to the Revolution. If Poland was the salvation of France from its enemies, who were gathered together ostensibly to overwhelm the Revolution, the Revolution in France may be said to have been the cause of the undoing and dismemberment of Poland.

CHAPTER IX

THE OUTBREAK IN POLAND

As soon as the Empress Catherine had made herself mistress of Poland, and had come to terms with Prussia as to the districts to be assigned to it, she turned her restless and devouring ambition in the direction of Turkey. The Emperor Francis had already been suggesting to her common action against that decadent Empire. With this object she directed the greater part of her army, then in occupation of Poland, to march eastward, and to concentrate on the River Dneister. There remained not more than 20,000 of her troops under General Igelström, rather more than half of whom were quartered at Warsaw. The whole of the Russian army had been maintained at the cost of the Poles. Its soldiers had supplemented their meagre pay and food by wholesale maraudings and extortions. Everywhere discontent was rampant. Secret societies multiplied and insurrection became imminent.

Kosciuszko, who had been in exile in Germany since the defeat of the Polish army, was chosen as leader of the new national movement in Poland. He paid secret visits to it, and organized an outbreak. He also opened communication with the Convention in Paris, and received encouragement from them, and some small contributions in money towards the Polish cause. It was obvious to him that the outbreak ought to be postponed, till the Russians were completely involved in war with Turkey. The news, however, of French victories, at the close of 1793, greatly stimulated the national movement in Poland, and raised hopes that Austria and Prussia would find their hands full, in the war with France, and would be unable to lend assistance to Russia.

A wave of popular enthusiasm spread over Poland. The immediate cause of outbreak, however, was the treatment by the Russians of the Polish army. At this time, after the second partition, the army consisted of about 30,000 men. The Empress, informed as to the spread of disaffection among them, gave orders that it was to be reduced to 13,000 men, of whom

7,000 were to be in Lithuania, which had been incorporated as a Russian province, leaving 6,000 only for the rest of Poland. The men dismissed from service in the Polish army were to be allowed to volunteer into the Russian army. The operation of disbanding was delayed for some weeks by the refusal of the Diet to give its consent. It was not till the middle of March 1794 that this was forced upon them. In some few places it was carried through without difficulty, and the disbanded men, who without exception refused to volunteer into the Russian army, found their way to Warsaw, where they added to the elements of disturbance. But at Pultusk, in the Cracow district, ten squadrons of Polish cavalry, under General Madalinski, refused to obey the order to disband, and raised the standard of revolt. This precipitated a general insurrection throughout the country. General Igelström thereupon sent Generals Donnislaw and Thomasson, with 7,000 men from Warsaw, to quell the revolt, under Madalinski.

Meanwhile Kosciuszko, hearing of the Polish revolt, hastened from Dresden to Cracow, and arrived there on March 25, 1794. He found that the Polish battalion there had driven out the small Russian garrison. As the Polish army was necessary for his scheme, he recognized that the insurrection must be proceeded with, in spite of the fact that war had not actually commenced between Russia and Turkey. He assumed command of the Polish army, and issued a patriotic manifesto calling upon the Poles to fight for their country. He announced that he would assume dictatorship in Poland, and form a Government. His appeal was everywhere received with enthusiasm, and the troops and citizens of Cracow took an oath of allegiance to him. The movement rapidly spread throughout Poland and Lithuania. It was not, however, supported by many of the great landowners, who feared the spread of revolutionary principles among their serfs. But the *petite noblesse* to a man joined in it, as did also the burghers of Warsaw and other towns.

On April 29th Kosciuszko, hearing that Madalinski was hard pressed by General Thomasson, left Cracow with 2,000 men, hastily raised in support of him. On joining Madalinski they formed a force of 4,000 men, one-half of whom were peasants, armed only with scythes. On May 4th, at Raclawitz, they met General Thomasson, with an equal number of men, all of them trained soldiers, and with a number of guns. Kosciuszko showed great vigour and skill. He attacked the centre of the Russian force with the bayonet and scythe, and drove them back with great slaughter. His peasants charged the Russian batteries, and mowed down the gunners with their scythes. The Russians retreated with great loss. Kosciuszko himself was compelled to retire to Cracow after the battle, in consequence of the disorder and plight of his cavalry. But the honour of the day rested with him.

This engagement was followed by an outbreak at Warsaw, where Igelström endeavoured to disarm the Polish troops. After two days of desperate fighting in the streets, the Russians were defeated, and were driven from the city on April 18th, with the loss of more than half their force. Igelström showed no capacity for dealing with such an *émeute*. At the earliest symptom of an outbreak he had packed off his furniture and his mistress to Russia. But he made no arrangements for concentrating his men, or for defending the arsenal, and preventing the insurgents from supplying themselves with arms and gunpowder. The

Russian troops had fallen into bad discipline and showed no power of cohesion and resistance. After the fall of Warsaw, the outbreak became general throughout Poland, and the Russians were compelled to evacuate it. Kosciuszko found himself master of the whole country. Stanislaus gave in his adhesion to the provisional Polish Government and remained at Warsaw. But he was as much a nullity as he had been under his late masters, the Russians.

When the Empress Catherine heard of this outbreak she was consumed with anger against the Poles. She made up her mind to avenge herself on them, to destroy, once for all, what little vestige of independence remained to them, and to effect their complete subjection, by incorporating the greater part of the country in the Russian Empire, and sharing the remainder with Austria and Prussia. She did not feel strong enough to effect this alone. She called upon these two Powers to perform their treaty obligations of assisting her against the Poles. Fortunately for her schemes, she had not so far committed herself to war with Turkey as to be unable to abandon, for the time being, her ambitious scheme of aggrandizement in that direction. She gave orders that terms were to be come to with the Turks, as soon as possible, and that the army under Suwarrow, when this was effected, was to march to Poland.

The outbreak occurred at a bad time for the Polish cause. The Empress, it has been shown, was not as yet entangled in actual war with the Turks. Austria and Prussia, for different reasons, had become lukewarm in support of the war with France, and were not sorry to have an excuse for turning their attentions in another direction. The Emperor Francis was hoping to take part with Russia in the war against Turkey, with a view to territorial aggrandizement in that direction. The King of Prussia, having secured his share of Poland in the recent partition, and having fought a campaign against France, at the instance of the Empress, in order to secure this share from her, was not eager to assist Austria in retaining or regaining Belgium, where he had nothing to gain except glory in defeating the Jacobins.

But for the efforts of the British Government, and the hope of large subsidies for carrying on the war with France, it is probable that the coalition would then have been dissolved. Already, before the outbreak in Poland, Lord Malmesbury, in December 1793, had been busily engaged, on behalf of the British Government, in urging the Prussian King to embark on another campaign against France. He found great difficulty in this, not on the part of Frederick William himself, who was willing enough to continue his crusade against the French Revolution, but on the part of his principal advisers, military and civil, and his backstairs advisers, who were almost unanimously opposed to a renewal of the war with France.

The Duke of Brunswick, who resigned in January his post as Commander-in-Chief of the Prussian army, his successor, Marshal Möllendorf, Schulenberg, the Chief Minister, and Lucchesini, who had great influence with his master, and who was now Ambassador at Vienna, used their utmost efforts to persuade the King against continuing the war. It is probable that they did not object to his taking a subsidy from England, for that brought grist to their mill. There was great want of this. The Treasury was depleted, and there were not the means to pay the troops or even to provide them with food and equipment for war.

Malmesbury, after long negotiations, succeeded in effecting, on April 19, 1794, at The Hague, a treaty between England and Holland on the one hand and Prussia on the other. By this Prussia undertook, in return for subsidies, to put 62,000 men into the field, properly equipped for war, in addition to the 20,000 men already assembled at Mainz, its contingent to the army of the Empire. These additional men were to be at the disposal of England and Holland, for another campaign against France to put down its anarchical Government. They were to be ready at Mainz by May 24th. The plan of the campaign was to be decided by a military convention. For this £300,000 was to be paid in a lump sum in ready money and £50,000 a month, and money for food and forage, calculated at the monthly rate of £1 12s. per head for 82,000 men.

On April 30, 1794, Pitt asked the House of Commons to vote the sum of £2,600,000 for the purpose of giving effect to this subsidy to Prussia. Charles Fox made a vehement attack upon it.

"The demand of Prussia [he said] amounted to this: 'I have got England and Holland into this contest with France. They are involved in it from my adventure. I will discontinue my efforts unless they choose to bear my expenses.' It was scarcely possible for the mind of man to conceive conduct more odious. It was a mixture of fraud, perfidy, and meanness perfectly new in modern political history. So infamous had been the conduct of the King of Prussia that it was impossible for any man of the least prudence to trust that Court in any way. He would ask the House whether the perfidious conduct of the Court of Berlin to France and Poland was a sufficient motive to induce us to place implicit confidence in its future adhesion to the faith of treaties." *

He predicted that Prussia would play false, and that the money would be thrown away. The House of Commons, at the instance of Pitt, voted the money by a large majority. But the prediction of Fox was soon verified. It will be seen that the Prussian Government, while pocketing the subsidies, never moved a single step towards carrying out their part of the bargain.

The correspondence of Lord Malmesbury shows that the ink was scarcely dry on the treaty, before the Prussian Ministers began to raise difficulties in giving effect to it. Some short delay took place in the actual payment of the cash by the British Government. The Prussians, in spite of the assurance of Malmesbury that the payment was as certain as if

* *Parliamentary History*, September 30, 1794.

the money was actually in their Treasury, took advantage of this to delay giving orders for the assembling of troops at Mainz. When the money was paid they objected to their army, when assembled, being employed in Flanders. In vain did Malmesbury point out the precise terms of the treaty, and assert that the very basis of it was that the Prussian troops, in return for their subsidy, should be employed, in concert with the armies of Austria and England against France. In a dispatch to Grenville in August, after consultation with the Prussian Ministers, Malmesbury wrote:—

> "Haugwitz [the Minister who negotiated the treaty] is a nullity. Lucchesini rules despotically; and as he did not negotiate the treaty he now opposes its execution in every possible way. General Möllendorf is a dotard. Nothing remains of him but his vanity."

And, again complaining of the ill-feeling of the Prussians, he added:—

> "It required more suspicion than I wish to possess, and more penetration than I have any claim to, to suppose there could exist such a total disregard of public character and sound feeling. I declared to Hardenburg that the King [George III] does not and will not recognize the right of disposing of the future movements of the Prussian Army, otherwise than according to the express and unquestionable meaning of the treaty." *

* Lord Malmesbury's *Memoirs*, ii. p. 113 *et seq.*

All these protests of Malmesbury were unavailing. There never was any intention, on the part of the Prussian Ministry, to carry out the terms of the treaty. Of the 62,000 additional troops to be assembled at Mainz, not more than 20,000 were sent there. There was distinct refusal to allow them to be sent to Flanders, or to be used otherwise than in defence of the German Empire. The force assembled at Mainz was, in fact, insufficient for the purpose of an advance against France, in concert with the Austrian and British armies.

The main cause for this disregard by Prussia of the obligation under the treaty of The Hague was to be found in the Polish outbreak. When the news of it arrived at Berlin the King's advisers pressed on him, with more insistence than ever, the necessity for withdrawing from active operations in Flanders and on the Rhine. The conflagration in Poland, it was said, would certainly extend to the adjoining Prussian province of Posen. Prussia, therefore, must arm in that direction. She must be prepared for decisive measures. If she were to assist in putting down the revolt, and in occupying Cracow, she would be able to take up a dignified and decisive attitude on the Polish question. It was impossible for her to carry on war at the same time both on the Rhine and the Vistula. The withdrawal, therefore, of Möllendorf from the French theatre of war was a necessity. It would be useless for Prussia to sacrifice herself for England and Austria.

These arguments had no immediate effect on the Prussian King. He had very recently signed the treaty with England. He wished, no doubt, to pocket the subsidies. He still personally hoped to gain glory and honour by putting down the French Revolution. He was vehemently hostile to anything savouring of France. He had even denied himself the luxuries of French cooks and French *danseuses* in his theatre. He could not give up the chance of inflicting vengeance on the regicides at Paris. He intended to take command himself of his army in the west for this purpose. For the present, therefore, he turned a deaf ear to the suggestions of treachery to England. But, in view of the threatened danger to his Polish provinces, he was persuaded to give orders to mobilize an army on his eastern frontier.

Later, when the outbreak in Poland had

further developed, Frederick William began to waver. It was represented to him by his advisers that his presence with the army, on the Polish frontier, was urgently needed, and that he must abandon his project of taking command of the army in the west. Austria, it was suggested, should be called upon to fulfil the terms of her treaty, and to send 20,000 men in support of Prussia against the Polish insurgents. If she refused, as was almost certain, Prussia would be justified in withdrawing 20,000 men, under Möllendorf, at Mainz, and sending them to reinforce the army in the east. To the renewed proposal that he should make peace with France, in order to devote the whole of his efforts in Poland, the King still opposed a determined veto. But further persuasion by his Ministers and Generals ultimately produced its effect. He abandoned his intention to join his army in the west, and on May 14th he decided to leave Berlin for Posen, in order to take command of his army in the east. Möllendorf, at the same time, was instructed to be ready to send 20,000 of his men from the Rhine to Poland. This was a first, and perhaps the most important, step on the part of the King, towards withdrawing from the coalition against France. Two months later, when he was with his army before Warsaw, Lucchesini and others again renewed their efforts to induce him to come to terms of peace with France. The King still obstinately refused to do so. "No one," he said, "shall drive me to take so dishonourable a step as negotiation with regicides. How could I look England in the face, who is paying me subsidies? I shall be branded as a traitor to the Empire by Austria, who denies all separate negotiations. It would certainly be a fortunate thing if we had peace, but how can we obtain it honourably, before the Jacobins have felt the weight of our sword? No servant of mine shall induce me to take this first step." *

It will be shown that a very few months later Frederick William did what he thus pronounced to be dishonourable. He entered into negotiations with the Government of France for terms of peace, without the knowledge of his Allies, and later withdrew from the coalition, without having made any Jacobins feel the weight of his sword. Meanwhile he adopted a course which most people must think to be not less dishonourable: that of pocketing the subsidies

* Sybel, iv. p. 108.

of England, while persistently refusing to perform any part of the obligation under the treaty in respect of which the subsidies were paid to him. Malmesbury was indignant to the last degree. After ineffectual efforts to bring the Prussian Government to a sense of their duty under the treaty, he advised his own Government in London to discontinue payment of the monthly subsidies to Prussia. On October 25th, he was directed by Mr. Pitt to inform the Prussian Government that no more money would be paid to them. The Prussian Government thereupon had the assurance to denounce the treaty of The Hague, as though the breach of it was due to the British Government, and not to themselves. From a statement made in the House of Commons it appeared that the total of the subsidies paid by the British Government to Prussia, during the five months of the subsistence of the treaty, was £1,200,000, the full amount payable, on the basis of 62,000 additional men being assembled at Mainz. As no more than 20,000 additional men were ever assembled there, and these were in a short time transferred to Poland, by the direction of Frederick William, it followed that almost the whole of the above large amount of British money was expended in equipping, paying, and feeding Prussian troops, engaged, not in putting down the French Revolution but in stifling the outbreak in Poland and in the bringing about of its final dismemberment. It need hardly be said that no part of the money thus diverted from the purpose for which it was paid, was ever repaid to the British Government. A more dishonourable transaction it would not be easy to imagine.

CHAPTER X

THE TREACHERY OF AUSTRIA

THE policy of Austria at this juncture, in its ultimate result, was not very different, or less dishonourable than that of Prussia, though her withdrawal from the campaign in Flanders was longer deferred. When Thugut, the chief adviser of the Emperor, heard that Prussia had sent troops to assist the Empress Catherine in Poland, he was consumed with jealousy and distrust. He had, for some time past, been opposed to a continuance of the war with France. He did not value the Belgian provinces, at all events in comparison with the territorial aggrandizement of Austria in Poland, Turkey, and Italy. He regarded them as millstones round the neck of Austria. He was determined, if possible, to make peace with France. His policy is revealed to us in a dispatch which he sent, on April 10, 1794, to Cobenzl, the Austrian Ambassador at St. Petersburg, after hearing of the

Polish outbreak, and of the action of Prussia in sending troops there.

"Still worse," he wrote, "than the fear of the Polish insurgent is my dread of new measures of Prussian dishonesty and turbulence. The Prussian troops have begun their march towards Poland, and General Igelström makes no protest, but enters into an understanding with them. But we can by no means allow the Prussians to remain for any length of time in Poland, still less to take up a position in Cracow. The Emperor desires no change, and no acquisition in Poland, but only the right of garrison in certain border fortresses. But all this would be changed by a fresh aggrandizement by Prussia. Russia will know how to prevent this, and we beg to be informed of what she intends to do in opposition to Prussian rapacity. Reinforcement of the Russian army is the first thing to be done; and then—in the name of Heaven!—postponement of the Turkish war. The Emperor approves of the Russian plans and is ready to co-operate for their fulfilment; but at this moment the war with Turkey would be fatal, and Prussia would forthwith attempt new encroachments. Austria, in order to oppose her, would be forced to make peace with France on any terms. Above all, we must be fully assured that Russia will not share her favour between us and Prussia. If Russia were to allow Prussian troops in Poland, we too should have to march in to secure our portion in the last partition." *

The policy thus indicated, however, could not be carried out at once. The Emperor Francis was still, for the time being, intent on

* Sybel, iii. p. 439.

maintaining his Belgian provinces, and still hoped to put an end to the revolution in France. A large Austrian army, therefore, was collected on the Belgian frontier of France for the campaign of 1794, in front of Maubeuge, the failure to take which had been the last scene in the previous campaign of 1793. A mixed army of British Hanoverians and Dutch, under the Duke of York, was also there, but as it was now recognized that the Duke was not competent for a wholly independent command, this army was placed under the command of the Austrian Commander-in-Chief, the Prince of Coburg. The French, on their part, by a desperate effort of the Committee of Public Safety, of which Carnot was the leading spirit so far as military measures were concerned, concentrated a somewhat larger army to meet the Allied forces. It was, however, inferior in point of discipline and experience, especially as regards its cavalry. It was commanded by General Pichegru. Among its principal officers were Moreau, Regnier, Souham, and Macdonald, soon to become famous.

On April 1st, the Emperor and his two brothers, one of them the Archduke Charles, who later so distinguished himself as a General against Napoleon, left Vienna for Belgium, where later Thugut met them. On the 14th they joined Coburg's army at Valenciennes. The campaign of 1794 then commenced. The Emperor took command of the Allied army in person, but as he was eminently unfit for the position, Coburg virtually continued in command, subject to the interference of the Emperor and his Staff on critical occasions for political motives. The Allied army consisted of 162,000 men, of whom 45,000 were British, Dutch, and Hanoverians.

For a short time everything went well with the Allies. On two memorable occasions, at Villers en Cauchet, on April 24th, and at Le Cateau, on the 26th, the British and Austrian cavalry covered themselves with glory, by shattering large bodies of French infantry with great slaughter. The main armies, however, came into serious conflict for the first time at Turcoing on May 16th to 18th. In the meantime, news had arrived of the further development of insurrection in Poland, and of the expulsion of the Russians from Warsaw. The Empress Catherine was in serious alarm, and intimated to Thugut, through the Austrian Ambassador at St. Petersburg, that if the

Emperor would lend assistance in putting down the insurrection a very ample share of Poland, when reconquered, would be awarded to him. This was proof that another and final partition was in contemplation. A Prussian army was already at hand in the Posen district ready to help Russia. It was known that reinforcements were on their way to it, and that the King of Prussia was intending to take command of the army in Poland. It was very certain that if Austria did not assist in putting down the revolt of the Poles, the partition would take place without regard to her interests. Thugut, therefore, madly jealous and suspicious of Prussia, was more eager than ever to bring the war with France to a conclusion. Overtures of a confidential kind were received from the French Government about this time, with a suggestion of terms, which were not unfavourable, and which would have resulted in the retention of Belgium by Austria.

The British Government, who now aimed at the destruction of the Convention in Paris and of the Revolution, stood in the way of peace. Thugut did his best by intrigues with the Emperor to overcome this difficulty. An important section of the Imperial Staff, including

Prince Waldeck and General Rollin, who had great personal influence with the Emperor, agreed with him. This treacherous clique felt that success of the Austrians in Flanders would draw the Emperor further from Poland. Coburg and General Mack, who had drawn up the plan of campaign for the Emperor, were of the opposite opinion.

It was under the conditions of these divided counsels that the battle of Turcoing was fought. The Austrians had 90,000 men on the field, the French only 70,000. In spite of this disparity, the battle resulted in a defeat to the Allies, which practically decided the fate of the campaign. Of six columns of the Allied army, two, consisting mainly of British, Dutch, and Hanoverian troops, under the command of the Duke of York and General Otto, were overwhelmed, within easy reach of the remaining two-thirds of the army, composed wholly of Austrian troops, without any attempt on their part to render assistance, or to avert defeat. The order for the disastrous manœuvre was given directly by the Emperor, on the advice of his General Staff. In spite of the vehement protest of the Duke of York that it was certain to lead to defeat, the order was reiterated and insisted upon by the Emperor. The Duke then obeyed, with the result that the two columns were sacrificed, and the battle was completely lost to the Allies. York's columns were only saved from annihilation by their tenacity and courage in retreat.

Mr. Fortescue, in his admirable *History of the British Army*, has given a detailed account of this unfortunate battle, which, after the lapse of more than a hundred years, has for the first time been drawn from the records of the War Office and other sources. He suggests, as the only possible explanation of the disastrous order, that it was "dictated by wanton and deliberate wickedness" and was "prompted by political motives." "It may be asked," he says, "what the rest of the army was doing, while the two columns, together less than one-third of the whole, were in process of annihilation. The answer is that for some reason it preserved a conspiracy of inaction. Their torpidity was not unexpected or disapproved at headquarters." He concludes that the true reason was that Thugut was sick of the war in Belgium, and wished the British to be sickened of it also. "The decisive battle in the campaign," he asserts, "was lost by the deliberate design of the Imperial Staff and Government." *

Sybel also comes to much the same conclusion. "The Emperor's resolution to sacrifice his Allies and spare his own troops inexorably determined the fate of the campaign and the victory of France. . . . If, as we may suppose, the Prince of Waldeck procured the decisive order, he gained thereby a point of the greatest importance to his whole political system, for he thereby brought the Belgian war into such a position that he might, with unanswerable arguments, advocate the necessity for a retreat." † He suggests that Thugut was mainly responsible for the disaster, and that it was part of a deliberate scheme for overcoming the zeal of the Emperor against France, in view of the Polish position and his jealousy of Prussia.

A careful examination of the details of this disastrous affair must confirm the conclusions of these two historians, who alone have attempted to give an explanation of the extraordinary manœuvres of the Austrians in this battle. Their view is confirmed by what followed. Immediately after the battle of Turcoing the progress of the outbreak in

* Fortescue, iv. p. 270. † Sybel, iii. p. 435.

Poland had still further influence on the counsels of the Imperial headquarters. On May 23rd General Mack resigned his post as Chief of the Staff, disgusted by the failure of his elaborate plans. He was succeeded by Prince Waldeck, who, we have seen, was a partisan of Thugut, and was, like him, in favour of bringing the war in Flanders to an end, even if it involved the abandonment of Belgium. On May 24th, a Council of War, summoned by the Emperor, advised him that it was useless to attempt the further defence of Belgium. The Duke of York alone dissented from this. No immediate action was taken on this. But on the 28th, the Emperor decided to quit the army and return to Vienna. He gave as a reason that he wished to hasten the recruiting of his forces. No one believed this. His real reason was that Thugut's policy had prevailed with him, that it was necessary for him to deal with the Polish question, and to prevent Prussia getting the better of him in the partition which was certain to follow on the suppression of the revolt of the Poles.

The Emperor's withdrawal caused the most profound discouragement to the army which he left behind him. Coburg tendered his resignation, and was with difficulty persuaded to remain in command. Two-thirds of the Austrian officers tendered their resignations. The Allied armies, however, fought on with varying fortune, but in the main were compelled to retreat. On June 26th the battle of Fleurus was fought, where the Allies were again completely defeated. It decided irrevocably the campaign, and freed Belgium for ever from Austrian rule. Later, on July 29th, the Austrian army under Coburg separated from that under York, and retreated towards the Rhine, pursued by Jourdan. The Duke of York, with his British and Hanoverian troops, crossed the frontier into Holland. Instead of finding themselves in a friendly country, whose army was ready and willing to assist against the invading French, it was exactly the reverse. A popular movement among the Dutch people, in favour of the French, subverted the Government of the Prince of Orange, and drove him from the country. The Dutch army made no resistance to the French when they crossed the frontier in pursuit of York's army. Their fortresses everywhere surrendered to the enemy. The Dutch fleet, frozen up in the Zuyder Zee, allowed itself to be captured by a squadron of French cavalry. The British army was everywhere treated as an enemy. The country people refused supplies to it. The towns shut their gates upon it. Pursued by the French, under Pichegru, and driven from post to post, the British army made a disastrous retreat through Holland during the winter months, and after suffering untold miseries and frightful losses, found its way across the Prussian frontier to Bremen, whence, in the month of April, 1795, what remained of it was conveyed by transports to England.

Looking broadly at this campaign of 1794, it is clear that the Allied cause never had a chance of success. Prussia was false throughout. She gave no assistance whatever to the main objects—the defence of Belgium against the French, and the invasion of France for the purpose of putting down the Revolution. She took the money of England for these purposes, and spent it on the troops which were employed in Poland. Austria began the war with more vigorous intentions for her ostensible objects; but under the Machiavellian policy of Thugut she contrived the defeat of her Allies at Tourcoing, in order that the Emperor might be induced to abandon Belgium, and devote his energies to territorial aggrandizement at the expense of Poland.

Whether, if Prussia had performed her promise of putting 62,000 men at the disposal of England, and these men had taken part in the campaign in Flanders, and if Austria had also acted in good faith, and had put forward her full strength in defence of her Belgian provinces, and, when this was secured, in the invasion of France, and if England had been blessed with a competent War Minister and had also put forth her full strength in Flanders instead of frittering it away in futile expeditions all over the world, the objects aimed at would have been achieved, may be open to doubt. The magnitude of the peril to France roused it to incredible exertions. The diversion caused by the Polish insurrection came fortunately to its aid, and led to the failure of the Allied armies. Austria, though she lost her Belgian provinces, gained it will be seen, an equivalent of greater value to her in Galicia. Prussia, which had nothing to gain in the west, ultimately acquired a large addition to her Polish province, but lost to France her possessions on the left bank of the Rhine. England suffered more than her Allies in the disasters to her army while retreating through Holland. Instead of saving the Belgians from French aggression, and preventing Holland from falling under French influence, the war resulted in the complete subjection of Belgium to France and in Holland being withdrawn from the coalition and brought into close alliance with France. As against this, England obtained a few West Indian colonies and drove France from nearly all that remained to her in India. But of all the countries concerned in these events, Poland was the main sufferer from the failure of the campaign of 1794 against France. It was very doubtful whether Russia alone, at that time, would have been able to put down the revolt in Poland and Lithuania. That, at least, was the fear of the Empress Catherine, when she made urgent appeals to both Austria and Prussia for their aid. These two Powers were equally unwilling to embark in war at the same time both in France or Flanders and on the Vistula. Both were equally greedy for territorial plunder, and were madly jealous and suspicious of each other. Both, with equal baseness and dishonour, extricated themselves from the campaign against France, with the object of taking part with Russia in the subjection and final partition of what remained of the unfortunate Poland.

CHAPTER XI

SUPPRESSION OF THE POLISH REVOLT

In view of recent experience of the vast resources of Russia in men and armaments, and of her power of rapidly concentrating hundreds of thousands, and even millions, of soldiers on her frontiers, whether in the east or the west, it is not easy for us in these days to understand the difficulty which the Empress Catherine found in collecting a few thousands of men to quell the revolt of the Poles. It has been shown that, at the outbreak, she had only 20,000 men in Poland and Lithuania. Of these, at least 6,000 had fallen in the disaster at Warsaw, and in the fight against Kosciuszko in front of Cracow. The Empress sent at once what soldiers she could gather together—a few thousands only—from neighbouring provinces, or direct from St. Petersburg viâ Riga; but she relied chiefly on reinforcements from the army under Suwarrow on the Dneister. These would not be free to march to Poland, until terms had been come to with the Turks, and the army would then have to march some hundreds of miles before reaching the seat of war.

It was not till June 28, 1794, that a final settlement was effected with Turkey, and that orders could be given to Suwarrow to commence his march; and though that General made extraordinary haste, it was not till September 6th that his army reached the frontier of Poland. The Empress meanwhile, fearing that the insurgents would gain strength by delay in quelling them, had found it necessary to call in the assistance of both Austria and Prussia. She wrote personally to Frederick William to claim his assistance under the terms of her treaty with him. In another letter of the same date to Nassau-Siegen, her Ambassador at the Prussian Court, she wrote: "Let there be no routine, no jealousies. There must be general and cordial union against the hydra in Poland, which is aimed chiefly against kings and their legitimate power." She wrote also to the Emperor Francis: "The time is come when the three neighbouring Courts must use their efforts, not only to extinguish the smallest spark of the fire which has been kindled in their neighbourhood, but also to prevent its ever being rekindled out of the cinders." *

As regards Prussia, when suggestions were made to the Empress that it would be well for the three Powers to come to terms as to the disposal of Poland, after the insurrection had been put down, she was very reserved. Her Minister, Markoff, when questioned on this point, replied by quoting the Russian proverb, "The hide of the bear cannot be disposed of till the animal is slain." This did not prevent her discussing the future more fully with the Emperor Francis. Markoff asked Cobenzl, the Austrian Ambassador at St. Petersburg, point-blank to say, without ambiguity, what his master wanted in Poland. The reply was that Austria would require two equivalents, one for the partition which had been effected in 1793, from which the Emperor had been unjustly excluded, the other for the intended partition. The two statesmen examined a map of Poland. "What can be done with the remainder of Poland?" said Cobenzl. "It will be best to partition the whole of it," said Markoff. He added that the Empress

* Sorel, iv. p. 93.

was willing to engage by a secret treaty to defend Austria against the menaces and usurpation of Prussia, whether in the matter of Poland or France.*

The Emperor Francis, before leaving Vienna for Flanders, on April 10th, wrote to Cobenzl: "If a new partition is inevitable, the Emperor will claim a suitable share, such as to compensate him for the successive aggrandizements of Prussia. And if the Prussians send their troops into Poland, the Emperor must do the same, and if Russia gives way to the Prussian usurpation peace with France will become a necessity."

Thugut also wrote that if Prussian cupidity should occupy itself with a new scheme of rapine, Austria would be bound to oppose it, and in such case would find it impossible to continue the war with France. He admitted the possibility that peace with France would be the only means of preventing the success of Prussia against the Poles. The Emperor, thereupon, gave orders to suspend the march of reinforcements to Flanders.

There was much reason for this distrust of Prussia, on the part of the other two Powers. Austria had only 18,000 men in Galicia, and

* Sorel, iv. 94.

could not well add to their numbers, so long as she was at war with France. Russia, as we have already shown, had difficulty in adding to her force in Poland until she had come to terms with Turkey. Prussia had no less than 50,000 men in Poland and in her Polish province, of which 18,000 were under General Favral in the district of Cracow. This concentration in Poland had been effected at the expense of the army on the Rhine, and by neglecting to fulfil the promise to England to send 62,000 additional men there for offensive operations against France, in concert with the Allied armies in Flanders.

The King of Prussia arrived at the headquarters of General Favral, near Cracow, on June 3rd, and took personal command of the Prussian army. He was accompanied by Lucchesini and General Mannstein, the latter his chief confidential adviser on military affairs, a man of good common sense and clear perception. Prince Nassau-Siegen, the Russian Ambassador, joined him a few days later, and gave the latest information of the disposition of the Empress. He obtained a good deal of personal influence over the weak and vacillating mind of the King.

A force of 12,000 Russians, under the command of General Fersen, was in connection with the Prussian army in front of Cracow. It consisted partly of the remnant of the army which had escaped from Warsaw. The aggregate force, therefore, at the disposal of the King was, presumably, quite sufficient to defeat the insurgent Poles, and to capture Warsaw.

It was the ardent wish of the King and his advisers that Prussia should become possessed of the part of Poland lying to the west of the Rivers Narew and Vistula, including both Warsaw and Cracow. If the Prussian Army were able to defeat Kosciuszko, and capture these two cities, before Austria could come into the field, and before the arrival of the Russian reinforcements under Suwarrow, Prussia would be in the most favourable position of having possession of these coveted districts when the question of the final partition of Poland should be discussed between the three Powers. *Beati possidentes* was a maxim well understood in those days, as applicable to negotiations, and was not first invented by Bismarck. Lucchesini and Mannstein urged these considerations on the King, and pressed him to act with vigour and determination, and there can be little doubt that if he had followed their advice he would have been able to put himself into this favourable position.

On the other hand, Austria was quite determined that Cracow should not fall into the possession of Prussia. The Emperor looked upon the districts of Cracow and Sandomir as essentially necessary to him for the enlargement of Galicia. The Empress Catherine also was equally unwilling to allow the aggrandizement of Prussia to this great extent. Whatever prospects, however, the King of Prussia may have had of putting himself into the favourable position of actual occupation of these districts, by the defeat of the Poles, they were lost by his want of vigour and capacity as a General, when he had the opportunity of capturing Warsaw.

Frederick William was already, at the age of fifty, blasé and effete. He was ambitious, and had the predatory instincts of his race for territorial aggrandizement, but he had none of the vigour, determination, and self-confidence of his great predecessor. He was equally wanting in any sense of the difference between right and wrong in political actions. But whereas Frederick II restricted his villainies to great occasions, Frederick William II was habitually addicted to them in matters small as well as great. He had one of the worst defects of a ruler: that of distrusting his official advisers, and liking to show his independence and power by overruling them. But as he also distrusted himself, he fell into the hands of irresponsible and unscrupulous outsiders, and not infrequently of his mistresses, who were influenced by others in the background. He was entirely wanting in military capacity, and as he would not give free hands to capable Generals, he frequently ruined their plans by his interference. No one of them suffered more from this than the Duke of Brunswick, who had deservedly been reckoned as the ablest General of his time, but who lost the greater part of his reputation in the campaigns against France in 1792 and 1793, owing to the interference of the King. Complaining of this, the Duke said that he was never more than a nominal Commander-in-Chief, and was obliged in essential matters to yield to influences above him. "A King of Prussia," he wrote, "is not like a King of France, a Louis XIV, who left to the Prince de Condé or to Marshal Turenne the entire disposition of events. The Kings of Prussia are essentially a military family. In them centres during a campaign all the rays of the general direction, and the influence of a Commander-in-Chief is reduced to a reaction against them." *

Frederick William when in Poland showed all these defects in his character. It was essentially necessary for his policy that his army should capture Warsaw. Lucchesini and Mannstein in vain tried to hold him to this purpose. He fell under the influence of Nassau-Siegen, who pulled him in the opposite direction. He did not perceive that the interest and policy of the Empress were exactly the reverse of his own, and aimed at protracting the campaign, and preventing him from achieving the position of actual possession of the coveted provinces. It will be seen later how easily he might have made himself master of Warsaw if he had been endowed with a part only of the vigour of Suwarrow.

For a time, however, the King did well. On June 5th he received information that the Polish army, under Kosciuszko, was issuing

* *Life of the Duke of Brunswick*, by Lord Fitzmaurice, p. 63.

from Cracow. He gave directions that his army was to support the Russian General Denizoff in front of that city. Kosciuszko had formed a junction with General Growchowski. Their united force consisted of only 17,000 men, of whom only one-half were trained soldiers, and the other half hastily raised peasants, armed with scythes. The combined army, of Prussians and Russians, opposed to them, amounted to 37,000 men. There was little doubt as to the result. In spite of desperate valour on the part of the Poles, their army was completely defeated at Rawka. The peasants were routed and fled in all directions. Kosciuszko was able to retire with what he could save of his army towards Warsaw. Cracow fell into the hands of the Prussians on June 15th.

If the Prussian King had followed up this victory with vigour, there can be little doubt that he could have prevented the entry of Kosciuszko into Warsaw, and might have assaulted and captured that city without serious opposition. He delayed, however, in a most unaccountable way. It was not till a fortnight after the battle of Rawka, that he advanced with his army in the direction of Warsaw.

This gave time to Kosciuszko to rally what remained to him of his army, to add to its numbers by reinforcements from other districts, and to enrol fresh bands of peasants. With these he entered Warsaw, on July 9th. He was able to concentrate there no more than 17,000 soldiers and 13,000 untrained peasants. These with the citizens formed the garrison of Warsaw. There were 450 guns in the arsenal, which, by the negligence of General Igelström, had fallen into the hands of the insurgents. The city was practically undefended by permanent fortifications, but the citizens had been engaged for some weeks in making entrenchments. In Warsaw itself there were grave dissensions, which added to the difficulties of defence. There were three parties there. There was a small party in the interest of Russia, most of them in her pay, others expectant in the same direction. There was another party, of which the King Stanislaus was the leader, and to which most of the wealthy inhabitants belonged. Though they sympathized with the insurgents, and wished them success, they did not believe in their achieving it. They looked upon the cause as hopeless. They had no sympathy with the democratic views of the great majority of their fellow-citizens. They were regarded themselves with suspicion. The democracy insisted upon strong measures against the men who, as members of the Diet at Targowitz, had betrayed the Republic, and those who had voted for the treaties with Russia and Prussia in the Diet of Grodno. Seven of these were hanged by the mob. More would have been treated in the same way if Kosciuszko had not intervened forcibly, and directed similar measures to be taken against some of the men engaged in this work.

Kosciuszko, it has already been shown, was a man of very high qualities: calm and cool in the presence of great difficulties and dangers, inspiring great confidence in his military capacity, beloved by his soldiers, who called him Father Thaddeus, of irreproachable character, a most genuine patriot; but it may be doubted whether he possessed the power to deal with a position such as he found it in Warsaw. He had not the force of a Danton to inspire the populace with resolution, or the organizing power of a Carnot. He was more of the type of Lafayette. He had popular sympathies. He always wore a peasant's dress; but he refrained from rousing the enthusiasm of the peasantry, lest he should alienate the nobles. He chose his principal advisers from the moderate party, and became himself suspected by the democratic party. The two main parties in the city fought, side by side, in the trenches, and vied with one another in repelling the enemy, but at other times they glared at each other, full of suspicions of treachery or crime. The difficulties of defence under these conditions were great.

It was not till July 13th that the Prussian army appeared before Warsaw. Lucchesini and Mannstein strongly advised the King to direct an immediate assault on the trenches hastily thrown up by the citizens. A few weeks later, when time had been given for strengthening them, and when the defenders had learned by experience how best to repel attack, Suwarrow with a very much smaller force was able to carry these works by assault, and to capture the city. But Frederick William was of very inferior metal to the great Russian General. He allowed himself to be dissuaded by Nassau-Siegen, against his own better judgment, from this bold course. There can be little doubt that the Russian Ambassador had instructions from the Empress to delay the capture of the city, if possible, till the arrival of Suwarrow. Indeed, it has been suggested that she wished for the defeat and retreat of the Prussians, in order that she might intervene later with greater effect, and that the King of Prussia might not be in a favourable position, when the time should arrive for the final partition.

The advice of Nassau-Siegen prevailed, and the Prussian army sat down before the feeble defences of Warsaw, with the intention of carrying on a *siège en règle*. As neither the Prussians nor Russians had any siege-guns at hand, it was not till July 28th that their batteries were in a position to commence a bombardment. In the meantime the Prussians had found no difficulty in capturing Cracow, and possessing themselves of the Palatinates of Cracow and Sandomir, which they so much coveted. "Take whatever you can," was the advice of Lucchesini to the King, "so as to have something to give up which you don't want, and to keep the line of the Vistula." He again urged the bombardment of Warsaw, to be followed by an assault. It was argued against this by others that an assault, if unsupported, might compromise the Prussian army;

that it was most necessary to keep this intact, in order to restrain the Russians; and that, in any case, humanity forbade the Prussians from taking bloody revenge against a city which was soon to become Prussian.

Lucchesini about this time again urged the King to make peace with France. "If Belgium were left to the French," he said, "they, on their part, would consent to give up any territory they had already acquired in Germany, and thus the honour of the King would be safe. The army of Möllendorf when liberated in this way would become the arbiter in the partition of Poland." The King, however, refused to allow negotiations with the ruffians of the Convention. For his part, Lucchesini said that he had no objection to negotiate even with Robespierre.*

The siege of Warsaw was protracted. The Poles, in spite of their internal dissensions, defended the weak entrenchments with the utmost vigour and determination. As time went on the difficulties of an assault increased rather than diminished. Towards the end of August, Frederick William, encouraged by the success of his troops against some outposts

* Sorel, iv. 96.

of the Poles, and by their successful repulse of a sortie, made up his mind, at last, to attempt an assault, and arrangements were made for its taking place on September 1st. But just before that day he heard from St. Petersburg that the Empress strongly approved General Fersen's objections; and, fearing that the Russian troops would not support him, if the attack were made, he countermanded the assault. Lucchesini, unfortunately, had returned to his post at Vienna, and was not at the King's elbow to pin him to his original decision. The King was also alarmed by the spread of insurrection of the Poles in his own province of Posen. He feared lest his army should find itself between two forces. He did not appreciate the fact that the best way of putting down insurrection in Posen, or elsewhere, was to strike at the head of the whole movement at Warsaw. He decided to abandon his position before the city.

On September 5th, the siege of Warsaw was raised, and Frederick William was reduced to the humiliating course of retreating with the army to Posen before the insurgent Poles. A few days later he abandoned the army, and returned to Berlin in bad health and in the worst of tempers. Never was there a more striking illustration of the failure of a great military operation through infirmity of purpose, and want of resolution of the General.

The retreat of the Prussian army was not dissimilar to that which had been made from France after its repulse at Valmy. The retreating army avenged itself on the unfortunate districts through which it passed, by devastation, incendiarism, and extortions. The Russian army, under General Fersen, also retreated, but not in company with the Prussians. They took a direction where they hoped to meet Suwarrow. The Prussians must have been very badly informed as to the movements of their Allies, for already, by September 1st, Suwarrow was very near to the frontier of Poland, and if the King had waited a few days longer in front of Warsaw, he would have been reinforced by the Russian Army, and would have been spared the humiliation and discredit of a retreat before the Polish insurgents.

On September 15th Suwarrow arrived at Brzesc, on the River Bug in Lithuania, with 8,000 men, after a march of 370 miles in three weeks. Suwarrow was one of the most remarkable, original, and truly national soldiers whom Russia has produced. The son of parents in a good position, he had enlisted in the army in preference to following the profession of the law. He passed slowly through all the grades of common soldier, corporal, and sergeant, and only after fourteen years of service achieved the rank of lieutenant. He retained through life the habits and language he had acquired in the barrack-yard. He was much of a hero, but also in part a charlatan, a fanatic, and a mystic. He affected to despise the ordinary rules and science of war, but, in fact, he had studied its histories and its principles with good effect. He combined two great qualities of the utmost value to a General, illimitable patience and prudence in the earlier stages of manœuvres, and extraordinary vigour and pertinacity when the time arrived for striking. He inspired unbounded confidence in his soldiers. He never failed to lead them to victory and to booty. He did not spare them in marching or in fighting. He was absolutely reckless of life, when he was determined to strike and win. When he achieved victory he followed it up, without loss of a moment, and with relentless fury, till he had destroyed the last vestige of the enemy. His bold and successful assault on the Turkish town of Ismail, which other Russian Generals had failed to take, resulted in the massacre of the whole garrison and all the inhabitants, and filled Europe with astonishment, and his opponents with alarm. He was the idol of his soldiers. He liked to bandy jests with them. They appreciated still better his care for their food and clothes, in striking contrast to other Generals in the Russian army, who habitually made money at their expense. His battle-cry of attack was: "No long manœuvring, no long firing. Forward with the cold steel! Down with them all! Death to all of them!" The bold determination and self-confidence of the Russian soldier was the exact opposite to the faltering dilettantism of the Prussian King.

Within two days of his arrival at Brzesc Suwarrow attacked and utterly defeated and destroyed a Polish army of 10,000 men. Kosciuszko, when he heard of this, recalled General Dombrowski, who had been following the retreating Prussian army. He himself, with 8,000 men, issued from Warsaw to meet and engage Suwarrow, but hearing that General Fersen was on his flank, and being misled as to the strength of this Russian corps, he turned aside, in the hope of destroying it before Suwarrow came up.

The Russian army, in fact, greatly outnumbered that of the Poles. Fersen attacked Kosciuszko's army at Maciejowice and completely defeated it, on October 9th, in spite of prodigies of valour on the part of its General and men, one-half of whom were peasants. Of the 8,000 only 2,000 survived and returned to Warsaw. Kosciuszko, who made desperate efforts for victory, and showed great personal courage, having three horses killed under him, was wounded and taken prisoner. It is not true that he exclaimed on being captured, "*Finis Poloniæ!*" but not the less, the expression aptly described the effect of the defeat of the Polish army and the capture of its General. Kosciuszko was the one man who had impressed the whole of Poland. The defeat and capture of their Father Thaddeus caused a profound sense of discouragement. The peasants in most cases threw away their scythe-blades and dispersed.

General Dombrowski was able to withdraw his corps into Warsaw. Another Polish army was defeated and destroyed by Suwarrow on his march to Warsaw. Immediately after this battle Suwarrow wrote to the Prussian General Schwerin: "As soon as Derfelden has joined me, which he must do in a few days,

I shall proceed, with firm step, to the decisive assault on Praga [a suburb of the capital]. Warsaw shall cease to exist. To see the insurgents wandering on the bank, to annihilate them, and to plant the standard of the mighty Empress as a fearful warning to the faithless city—that is my object."

It was in this spirit that Suwarrow followed up his victory. General Schwerin, in command of the Prussian army, refused or neglected to join him. General Derfelden effected a junction with him on November 1st, bringing up the total force of the Russian army to 22,000 men. Two days later they appeared before Praga, separated from Warsaw only by the Vistula. Suwarrow determined to assault it on the next day. Victory would necessarily give him command of Warsaw.

The Poles were greatly discouraged by the defeat of so many of their armies. General Makrokowski, who had been appointed successor to Kosciuszko, gave up his command in despair. Generals Dombrowski and Madalinski maintained a most gallant defence to the inevitable end. The earthworks of Praga were defended by 8,000 trained soldiers, 1,800 volunteers belonging to the suburb, and 2,000 citizens of Warsaw. At midnight of November 4th,

Suwarrow erected three batteries of eighty guns, and opened fire at three in the morning. The defenders of Praga, expecting only a bombardment, had not observed the Russian battalions which, in the night, had crept up to their lines. As soon as it was daylight the attack was made by the Russians in seven columns. The battle-cry was "Remember Warsaw!" in recollection of the terrible losses to the Russians when driven from that city. By nine o'clock the assaulting columns had overcome all resistance and were in occupation of Praga. There followed a scene, similar to that at Ismail, of indiscriminate massacre of the Poles in the town, whether fighting-men or citizens, whether women or children; 10,000 of the men who had fought were slain and 2,000 of them drowned in the Vistula. The loss to the Russians was only 1,400. Suwarrow is said to have been deeply moved by the awful scene of bloodshed. He appears, however, to have suppressed his emotions, for it was not till late in the day that he tried to restrain the fury of the troops. He promised to the few Poles who remained in Praga that if they would lay down their arms he would grant personal liberty, and security for life and property. The same terms were offered to

Warsaw, which now stood at his mercy. On the 7th the city capitulated. Ten days sufficed to disarm the remaining Polish forces in the field. Generals Dombrowski and Madalinski, who had conducted the brave defence of Praga, with Ignacius Potocki and other leaders of the patriots in Poland, were sent to St. Petersburg, and there imprisoned, as was also Kosciuszko.

When the King of Prussia heard at Berlin of the capture of Warsaw by the Russians, and the practical suppression of the outbreak of the Poles, he gave orders at once that 20,000 of his troops in his Polish province were to be sent back to the Rhine. It seemed that he again contemplated more active measures in the war which he was still nominally waging against France, and for which he was still in receipt of subsidies from England. He hoped, perhaps, to recover some of the military reputation which he had lost in Poland. This, however, was only the last flash of the war flame of the unstable and wavering King. All his advisers in Berlin, civil and military, were against him. They were full of indignation against Austria. They did their best to induce the King to come to terms of peace with France. He was almost alone in favour of prolonging this war. In order to break down his will, the Ministers called in the aid of Prince Henry, the younger brother and trusted adviser of Frederick the Great, who had still great influence in Prussia. He was fanatically hostile to Austria. He looked on the war with France as suicidal to Prussia, and for the benefit only of Prussia's malevolent rival, Austria. Under his influence Frederick William finally gave way. He was induced to issue secret instructions to Baron Goltz to initiate a negotiation for terms of peace with Barthélemy, the agent of the French Republic.

CHAPTER XII

THE THIRD PARTITION (1795)

POLAND lay prostrate again before the proud and astute Empress to do as she willed with it. She had completely circumvented the vacillating King of Prussia. She had made use of him and his army, at a critical moment, when her own army of occupation in Poland had been defeated and driven from Warsaw, and when her main army, under Suwarrow, was not at hand and available. She had induced him, after his first success, and when in front of Warsaw, to refrain from assaulting it, and to protract the siege, till Suwarrow was able to bring up his army and take his place there. Though her forces in Poland were inferior in number to those of Prussia, they had taken the main part in defeating and dispersing the insurgents, and without the assistance of the Prussians had captured Warsaw, which, with superior forces, the Prussian King had failed to do. As a result, the Empress had all the best cards in her hand for the political game of partition which was now to take place. The King of Prussia, by his lack of energy and determination, had thrown away his cards, with the exception of one which was still of value to him, the possession of Cracow.

Already, some weeks before her final success against the insurgents, the Empress, with splendid confidence as to the future, had opened discussions with the two German Powers as to the dismemberment of what remained of Poland. On July 23rd she wrote to them that the fate of Poland must be settled by a common negotiation of its three powerful neighbours.

The King of Prussia, in answer to this invitation, sent Count Towenzein to St. Petersburg, as Ambassador, with the following instructions :—

1. That the coming partition of Poland was better justified than the two previous ones.

2. That it was certain that Austria would not remain inactive, but would hasten, after her military reverses in Belgium, to make peace with France, and to seek compensation in Poland, but that the Emperor, although he had sent a small corps to Lublin, could not compare his

claim with that of Prussia, who had employed all her forces in Poland.

3. Towenzein was, therefore, to demand for Prussia all the country between Silesia, West Prussia, and the Vistula. He was to suggest that a narrow strip of territory between Russia and Prussia should be constituted into a neutral principality, and should be offered to Suboff, Catherine's paramour, on condition of his giving support to Prussia against Austria, and of using his influence to secure for Prussia a further slice between the Baltic and the frontier of Courland, and some other concessions. It was also proposed that a similar principality should be set apart for Nassau-Siegen, the Russian Ambassador at Berlin. In other words, these two important personages, one of whom, it was thought, would have great personal influence with the Empress, and the other would have the conduct of the negotiations on her behalf, were to be secured in the interests of Prussia by splendid bribes.*

The Prussian scheme thus developed meant that, just as in 1793, the partition was to be between Russia and Prussia only, and that Austria was again to be left in the lurch.

* Sybel, iv. p. 151.

These instructions were given at the time when the King of Prussia had appeared with his army before Warsaw, and when he had every expectation of capturing that city off his own bat.

The Empress Catherine was in no haste to receive any communication from Towenzein. She allowed some weeks to elapse in the hope, no doubt, that the position would be improved for her, when Suwarrow's army reached Poland. Meanwhile, she did her best, through General Fersen, to induce the King not to assault Warsaw and otherwise to delay the siege. When news of the retreat of Frederick William and his army from the lines in front of Warsaw reached her, she was evidently delighted. Towenzein reported that at her levée, the Empress received him with malicious smiles, but would not vouchsafe a single word to him.

Later, when Towenzein, in a confidential manner, proposed the Prussian scheme in detail to Suboff, including the bribe of a principality out of the Polish territory, Suboff, to his great surprise, declined the offer, declaring that he was quite unworthy of such a lofty position, and that the constitution of such a duchy was quite unfeasible. Suboff was notoriously venal, but he had, perhaps, the unhappy example of Stanislaus in his mind, and preferred to remain an intimate member of the Imperial Household, rather than accept a precarious principality at a distance.

With reference to the main part of the scheme, Suboff dwelt on the necessity for rewarding Austria liberally for her exertions against the French republic, compensation for which, he said, could not be found elsewhere than in Poland. He also expressed the hope that a report that Prussia was negotiating peace with France had no foundation, as nothing would hurt the Empress so much as a breach by Prussia of its treaty of 1791 in this respect. Towenzein declared the rumour to be an unfounded calumny, though he must have known that at the very time all the statesmen and Generals of Prussia were urging their royal master to adopt this very course.

It is evident that, by this time, the Empress had practically made up her mind to favour Austria in the coming partition. While in that of the previous year she had excluded Austria, and had made a secret treaty with Prussia for a share of Poland, she now reversed her action, and made terms with the Emperor, conceding to him a large share, not indeed to the exclusion of Prussia, but in reduction of its exorbitant claims.

It appears that in the meantime, on September 11th, Thugut had sent instructions to Cobenzl at St. Petersburg for communication with the Empress. "Austria," he said, "has always regretted the partition of Poland as injurious to her interests. If such a partition is unavoidable, she must, of course, protect her own interests by claiming a share, so that she may not be altogether thrown into the shade by the perfidious Prussians." *

After dwelling on the insatiable demands of Prussia and their utterly unjustifiable nature, he went on to observe that his master, the Emperor, might still fairly ask for other compensation, corresponding to the Russian and Prussian acquisition in the second partition of Poland in 1793. This might either be in a district taken from France or another slice of Poland. He was to ask for Austria the parts of Poland north of Galicia, including Cracow and Sandomir, and further compensation in Venetia, namely, the territory formerly in the possession of Austria. This being conceded, he was to intimate that the more Russia appropriated

* Sybel, iv. p. 165.

of Poland, and the less that was left to Prussia, the better pleased the Emperor would be. In fact, his scheme would virtually leave nothing for Prussia.

The Empress in the main declared herself on the side of the Emperor in the contest which then arose for the plunder of Poland. She did not, however, go so far as Austria wished in her rejection of the Prussian claims. She did not think it wise to drive that Power to extremities. On September 30th, she decided that Austria should have the four southern palatinates of Poland, viz. Cracow, Sandomir, Lublin, and part of Chelm; that the Rivers Vistula and Bug should be her own boundary in the future, and that the residue, including Warsaw and Praga, as part of that city, should be the share of Prussia. As regards other claims of Austria elsewhere than in Poland she was very generous.

"Take half of France," she said to the Austrian Ambassador, "take Venetia, take Turkish lands. We have no objection—but in Poland the Bug must be our boundary." *

The Bavarian exchange was again mooted, though the Emperor, in his negotiations with

* Sybel, iv. p. 167.

England, had expressly disclaimed any intention in this direction. It seems that the aged Elector of Bavaria, in his dotage, was anxious to marry an Austrian Archduchess, and was now favourable to an exchange, though the next heir of the Elector, the Wittelsbach family, and the people of Bavaria were strongly opposed to the scheme. Russia was not unwilling, and by admitting Austria as a party to the treaty of 1793, practically recognized this claim. On the other hand, the Empress required that the Emperor Francis should provide assistance to her in any future attack on Turkey. Subject to these considerations, Thugut was ready to concede the claim of Russia to Volhynia, and to limit his demand for Polish territory to the four palatinates.

On October 30th, a formal reply was sent by the Empress to Towenzein to the effect that the partition of Poland could not be deferred, and that the settlement must be such as to avoid all jealousies on the part of the three Powers. Austria, she said, required Cracow and Sandomir as indispensable bulwarks of Galicia, and would never consent to their acquisition by Prussia. The Empress, therefore, asked Prussia to give up these palatinates. For herself, she said, her only wish was to preserve friendly relations by a clearly drawn line. She required for herself the territories north of the Vistula and the Bug. She practically admitted the claim of Prussia to Warsaw and the districts south of the Vistula, but rejected her demand for Cracow and Sandomir.

The Empress had decided in favour of Austria as between the two German powers. About this time there arrived news of the breach between England and Prussia, of the treaty of The Hague, the cessation of the subsidy from England, and the direction given by the King of Prussia to Möllendorf to withdraw his army from the Rhine. This gave rise to some sarcastic remarks from the Empress. Her Chancellor, Osterman, told Towenzein that "the Empress thinks that Prussia's renown is engaged in the French war; she thinks that Prussia ought not to show herself so dependent on English money; and she sees how right she was not to place any Russian troops at the disposal of so inharmonious a coalition." Osterman added, on his own part: "They have forgotten in Prussia the benefits of the treaty of 1793; they wish to overlook the fact that South Prussia is a sufficient compensation, not for one but for four or five campaigns. They arbitrarily pass over the distinct stipulations of the treaty, in which they promised to continue the war until the French Revolution was suppressed."

Meanwhile, the King sent a reply to the note of the Empress Catherine, insisting on the retention of Cracow. If that were denied to him, he said, he would prefer the continuance of the arrangement of 1793 without any new partition of Poland. A conference then took place at St. Petersburg between the representatives of the three Powers—Osterman, on the part of Russia, Cobenzl and Towenzein for Austria and Prussia—when the scheme of partition was ventilated and discussed. Towenzein, on behalf of Prussia, strongly objected. He would not concede Cracow, of which Prussia was in actual possession. Ultimately he said that unless Cracow was given to Prussia, the partition would be impossible, and that no other course remained than to leave Poland in the same position as it was after the last partition. Both the Russian and Austrian representatives protested against this. "The three Courts," said Osterman, "have acknowledged the partition to be necessary for their mutual preservation. Prussia herself was the first to moot the question, and to maintain the unavoidable necessity of partition. Poland," he said, "is dead, gone for ever, and the dead cannot be called to life again."

"We two are agreed," said Cobenzl to Osterman, "on all points. Let us draw up the protocol. Let us sign the treaty. If Prussia will not join in it, well and good; we can do without her." Towenzein made an indignant protest, and the meeting broke up in open conflict.*

The Empress, after the failure of this conference, was evidently determined to act upon the advice of Osterman, and to come to agreement with Austria, without the concurrence of Prussia. She gave instructions for two treaties with Austria alone. After further discussion they were signed on behalf of the two Powers on January 3, 1795. In the first of them, relating only to Poland, the preamble ran: "That Poland having been entirely subjected and conquered by the arms of the Empress of Russia, she has determined to arrange with her Allies for a complete partition of that State, which has shown an absolute incapacity to form a Government

* Sybel, iv. p. 174.

which will enable it to live peaceably under the laws or to maintain itself in independence." The treaty then went on to provide that Russia was to appropriate all Polish territory between the Rivers Vistula, Bug, and Pelica, which then had a population of about 2,000,000. Austria was to have the four Palatinates already referred to, with 1,000,000 inhabitants; and the residue, including Warsaw, and a population then numbering 900,000, was to be left to Prussia, if she cared to claim it. In consideration of these acquisitions, each of the Powers was to guarantee the possessions of the others. As soon as Prussia declared her adhesion to this treaty she was to receive the share allotted to her, with a similar guarantee from both the other Powers.

By the second treaty, the Emperor agreed to be a party to the Russo-Prussian treaty of 1793, under which the claim of Austria to the exchange of Belgium for Bavaria was recognized. The two Powers bound themselves to help each other, with all their forces, in the event of Prussia attacking either of them. The Emperor promised, in the event of war between Russia and Turkey, to co-operate in realizing the agreement made between Catherine and the Emperor

Joseph, in 1782, and especially to constitute Moldavia, Wallachia, and Bessarabia as an independent principality for some member of the Imperial Family of Russia. Austria, in such case, was to receive a Turkish province, as formerly destined for the Emperor Joseph. Additional compensation was also provided for Austria, in case the fortunes of war should result in the Emperor being unable to obtain indemnity for the war from France. In such case Russia admitted the claim of the Emperor to the territory wrongfully appropriated by the Republic of Venice. These agreements, distinctly hostile to Prussia, were kept secret from that Power.

Having come to these agreements with Austria, the Empress could afford to treat the King of Prussia with disdain and contempt. In a letter of rude tone and overbearing pride to Prussia, Osterman said that the Empress had heard, with the greatest astonishment, the proposal of the King of Prussia to preserve the existence of Poland. This was one of those wishes which might indeed arise in the heart, but the fulfilment of which could not be hoped for, because it was contrary to the nature of things. As a proof of the truth of these assertions, Osterman referred to the late outbreak in Poland, which had indisputably proved the necessity of partitioning so volcanic a territory. He passed in review the claims of the different Powers, and enlarged on the moderation and fairness of Austria. With reference to the claim of Russia to the lion's share of the booty, he said:—

"We may boldly affirm that the title of the Empress to her portion of Poland is not the work of a moment or of a chance but the creation of thirty years of labour, cares, and colossal efforts of every kind; we may affirm, that in comparison with these, Austria and Prussia have received as an unbought gift all the advantages which they have reaped and will reap in Poland."

He ended by some advice for the future:—

"Prussia," he said, "should consider that by ready assent and compliance she could strengthen her alliance with Russia, and thereby obtain greater advantages than by insisting, as hitherto, upon convenient frontiers. Such a course on the part of Prussia would not have the least influence on the general condition of Europe, while those chimerical hopes of peace with France, of which so much has been said of late, could have no result at all." *

Nothing was said in this severe admonition of the agreements which had actually been signed between Russia and Austria, but it must have been evident to the Prussian King that

* Sybel, iv. p. 178.

these two Powers were virtually in agreement against him. The effect, therefore, was to convince him that his true interests lay in agreeing to terms of peace with France as soon as possible. On January 28th he agreed to sign definite instructions to Goltz to come to terms with Barthélemy at Basle for this purpose. It was not till April 5, 1795, that the long and difficult negotiations which ensued were brought to a conclusion, and that a treaty of peace was signed at Basle. It practically conceded to France the left bank of the Rhine, and the surrender to that Power of the territory of Prussia in that direction. The French, on their part, gave up the territory which they had gained on the right bank of the river. Prussia, thereupon, withdrew altogether from the coalition against France. For the next ten years she kept herself aloof from the wars which England and Austria maintained against successive Governments of France.

The Empress Catherine, when she heard that the King of Prussia had given way to his Ministers, and was negotiating for peace, was very indignant. She sent a special emissary to the King of Prussia to urge him against this course, and she wrote personally to the

Duke of Brunswick, asking him to use his influence with the King in an opposite direction to that of "the perfidious Ministers by whom he was surrounded," and to persuade him to break off negotiations with the regicides, and to continue the war against the French Revolution in accordance with the terms of the treaty with her.*

The emissary and the letter arrived too late. In fact, the first news which the emissary of the Empress heard, on arriving at Berlin, was that the treaty with France had already been signed. The Prussian Ministers and the Prussian Generals were delighted, and no one more so than the Duke of Brunswick, on whom the Empress had counted. Great was the wrath of the Empress when she heard that peace was signed by the King of Prussia, in violation of his treaty with her. Equally irate was the Emperor Francis. These two potentates, therefore, were now determined to force their settlement of Poland on Frederick William, and to eject the Prussian army from Cracow. On July 6th Cobenzl wrote to Thugut to inform him that Russia would effect this by force of arms, if necessary, and asked for

* Sorel, iv. p. 290.

the co-operation of Austria. The Emperor agreed, and for this purpose assembled an army of 80,000 men on the northern frontier of Bohemia. The Empress Catherine also made great preparations for the increase of her army in Poland. Thugut instructed the Austrian Ambassador at Berlin, in concert with the Russian Ambassador, to communicate to the Prussian Government the terms of the treaty of January 3rd, hitherto kept secret from them. In doing so they declined to enter into any discussion. They called on the Prussian Government either to agree to the terms of the treaty or to reject them.

The Prussian Ministers thus brought to the brink of war, while furious at what they considered the duplicity of the two Powers, thought it well to give way. They advised the King that there was no other course open to him than to comply immediately with the demands of Austria and Russia. Some further attempt was made to secure for Prussia a part of the Palatinate of Cracow, and a small tongue of land between the Vistula and the Bug. In the course of these hagglings Osterman said that if Prussia should venture to attack Austria, Russia would support the latter with all its force, and that Austria would at once make peace with France, and direct all her armies to Poland.

On September 3rd, at a last Conference on the subject at St. Petersburg, Austria consented to give up the small tongue of land between the Vistula and the Bug, but refused all concessions as to Cracow. Towenzein again protested that Prussia would rather return to the frontier of 1793, and wait for the ferment in Poland which the new partition would give rise to. This, however, was but a *brutum fulmen*. On October 29, 1795, Towenzein was instructed by the King of Prussia to sign, on his behalf, the treaty of partition of January 3, 1795. The Prussian army was directed to withdraw from Cracow and the Palatinate of Sandomir, and to give way to Austria. On the other hand, the Russians withdrew from Warsaw, and the Prussians took possession.

By a secret article of the partition treaty the three Powers, "recognizing the necessity of abolishing everything which may recall the memory of the existence of a Kingdom of Poland," bound themselves never to include such a designation among their territorial titles. The Empress Catherine, "in recognition of the wise dispensation of Providence," gave orders that public thanksgivings were to be offered in all the Churches of Poland for the blessings thus conferred on the country. Stanislaus was now permitted, or rather was directed, to abdicate his throne. He did so by a formal Act on November 25, 1795. This Act was attached to the treaty of partition. His debts at Warsaw were paid, and he was accorded an adequate pension, to be paid jointly by the three Powers. After the death of the Empress he took up his abode at St. Petersburg, where he spent the remainder of an inglorious life.*

The third and last partition thus effected by the three Powers completed the destruction of the ancient Kingdom of Poland. In the result, Russia obtained the lion's share, namely, 181,000 square miles, with a population of about 6,000,000. Austria gained 45,000 square miles, with 3,000,000 inhabitants, and Prussia 57,000 square miles, and a population of 2,500,000.

The three partitions must be considered historically as parts of a single great transaction,

* Fuller details of the negotiations between the three Powers which preceded the third partition of 1795 are given by Sybel, iv. 151–85, and Sorel, iv. pp. 186–93.

by which it was intended to erase Poland for ever from the list of nations.

In awarding the blame for these nefarious proceedings the palm must be given to Prussia. Russia was all along, and had been for years past, the open and declared enemy of Poland. There was no secrecy in her policy. The Empress Catherine carried out the designs of Peter the Great, and for thirty years was engaged in the avowed task of subjecting and dismembering her unfortunate neighbour. The only question was whether it was best, in the interest of her Empire, to reduce Poland to the condition of an impotent and helpless dependency, while preserving its existing boundaries, or to admit the other two Powers to a share in the plunder and to incorporate the lion's share as a Russian province. The safety of Poland had hitherto consisted in the fact that it was a buffer State between the three great Powers, and that it was not to the interest of two of them, Austria and Prussia, that Russia should be brought up to their frontiers.

However much we may condemn the public morality of Catherine's actions, it is impossible not to accord a tribute of amazement to the skill with which she pursued her objects. What a stroke of genius and cunning it was to embroil Austria and Prussia in war with France, so as to free her own hands for the accomplishment of her purpose! How cleverly she played off the one against the other, bribing first Prussia and later Austria with the plunder! And what skill she showed in the directions to her diplomatic agents and Generals!

With Prussia it was very different. Her course throughout these transactions was pursued with underhand perfidy, treachery, lying, and fraud, without example or precedent in history. There was this much to be said in mitigation of our judgment of Frederick II, for the first partition, that the separation of East Prussia from Brandenburg and other parts of his dominions made it a matter of great importance to his country to obtain the intervening province of West Prussia, the more so as one half of it was inhabited by Germans. If, however, he had waited, there would probably have arisen opportunities of obtaining the German half of the province by arrangement with Poland, in return for protection afforded to it against its other foes.

What made his policy specially nauseous was, that in order to gain for his own country a comparatively small territory, he tempted the two other Powers by offers of shares in the much larger plunder of an unoffending neighbour. On his own admission, in his letter to Solms above quoted, one of his main objects in persuading Austria to take part in the dismemberment of Poland was that he himself might not be involved in the universal odium which he knew would be incurred by him, if Prussia alone was concerned in the transaction. When, again, he gave way to Russia on the subject of Danzig and Thorn, he did so with the full belief that there would be another deal in the near future. He was much too clever a man not to perceive that his scheme would be the prelude to others of the same kind, and would necessarily lead to the ultimate extinction of Poland.

Whatever excuses may be alleged on behalf of Frederick, no plea can possibly be urged, on behalf of his successor, Frederick William, in abatement of his perfidies. In drawing Poland away from alliance with Russia, entering into a treaty, offensive and defensive, with her, promising support to her new Constitution, and then, when the ink of his treaty was hardly dry, turning round and throwing over all his treaty obligations, and agreeing with Russia to dismember Poland, his course was perfidious and disgraceful to a degree almost incredible. So also was his conduct to England in taking a large subsidy for an army to be employed in the war against France, and then refusing to perform his obligations, and using the army and the subsidy in dismembering Poland. His conduct to Austria in effecting the second partition, without securing to her the compensation he had promised, was equally underhand and dishonourable.

It may be well to consider how this conduct of Prussia has been dealt with by its patriotic historian. Sybel, with perfect honesty and truthfulness, describes most of the stages of dishonour, though not quite all, through which Prussia passed, and fully admits her utter perfidy, but he ends by justifying and defending it.

After narrating the second partition, the historian says :—

"It may seem harsh to expose the weakness of a perishing nation, but historical justice demands that we should not conceal the sins by which a people once powerful drew destruction on its own head. The melancholy spectacle of its fall would be more than we could bear if we were forced to regard it as the work of capricious fate and not as the consequence of deep and heavy guilt." *

Later, he adds :—

"The anarchy of Poland, which was the offspring of the unbounded licence of the nobility, avenged itself on its originators by inflicting upon them selfish frivolity and careless extravagance. . . ."

He proceeds to justify the action of Prussia :—

"The Court of Berlin had every reason, in 1793, to rejoice at the attainment of its object ; it was a conquest which was demanded by the most vital interests of self-preservation. . . . Moreover, from the progress which the German element had already made in the border district and the confusion of Polish affairs, it was to be hoped that the new Government would rapidly strike root ; the position of the monarchy, therefore, in the east might be regarded as settled on a sure basis. These aspirations, it is true, soon enough vanished in smoke ; and it has been a thousand times said that this failure was the necessary recompense of the perfidy and falsehood with which Prussia helped to trample down the freedom of her ally. We may be deceived by patriotic feelings, but we cannot refer the subsequent catastrophes to this source, however great the abhorrence we may feel for the acts of brutality which accompanied the event and the disregard of existing treaties. . . ." †

---

* Sybel, ii. p. 405. † Ibid., ii. p. 420.

"This much lies beyond doubt, that neither of the Polish parties had been guilty of any active aggression against Prussia, when she made up her mind to the partition. Prussia was, in every sense of the word, the aggressor against Poland, and that too without the shadow of a legal pretext. But if ever a policy of conquest was rendered desirable, nay, absolutely essential, by the circumstances of the times, it was in this case. . . .

"All things worked together—the deep corruption of the Polish State; the urgent necessity for Prussia to look after her own safety; and the general and impetuous advance of the other Powers. It is easy to point out the dark side in the resolutions come to in those perilous times; it is the duty of humanity to feel the deepest compassion for the fate of perishing Poland, but the question always remains, What better course was left to Prussia, considering the attitude assumed by Austria, Russia, and France? . . .

"After the most careful consideration, we can come to no other conclusion than this, that the resolution to appropriate a frontier province of Poland was decidedly the only one which, under the circumstances, did not lead to evident disaster—the only one, therefore, which was consistent with the duty of the Prussian Government." *

In the above passages the two main lines of a defence of Prussia are well defined. While admitting to the full the utter perfidy of his country, Sybel justifies it on the ground, first, that Poland by its misgovernment and by the tyranny of its ruling class of nobles had brought a just punishment on itself; and,

* Sybel, ii. p. 421.

secondly, that Prussia, in the interest of self-preservation, was forced to act as she did.

As to the first of these, Sybel takes the same line as Carlyle, without pushing it to the same extreme, or calling in aid the decrees of an Almighty Providence. It is sufficient to remark, on this part of the case, that Poland, in respect of the condition of its peasantry and the harshness of its feudal lords, was no worse than many of its neighbours at the time. The serfdom of the cultivators of the soil in Russia, Bohemia, Hungary, and most of the smaller States of Germany was hardly to be distinguished from that of Poland. As regards the anarchy of its Constitution, the historian omits to notice that Poland, if left to itself, would have provided a remedy, but that it was the settled policy of Russia and Prussia for many years to prevent reform; and that in 1763 these Powers bound themselves by treaty to use their armed forces to maintain the anarchical Constitution of Poland, with the express object of preventing her gaining strength to resist their predatory attacks. As regards the second, it need only be said that it is based upon the negation that in international relations there is any such principle as right, or justice, or honour, or good faith in treaties, and that the only true guide for action of one State to another is its self-interest, or what may seem to be its interest, at the time being. This, it must be admitted, has been the policy of the Hohenzollerns and their Ministers from the earliest times, through Frederick the Great and Bismarck down to the present time.

With respect to Austria, the third conspirator in the ruin of Poland, no one who studies the story can fail to be struck by the instability of her policy. During the twenty-three years from 1772 to 1795 four monarchs successively occupied her throne. There were as many changes of policy. The Empress, Maria Theresa, it has been shown, maintained as long as she could the traditions of the Hapsburgs by supporting the Kingdom of Poland; but in her old age she was over-powered by her son Joseph, and consented, against her moral sense, to join in the first partition. This must be considered as the action of Joseph, her successor, who was madly eager for territorial aggrandizement. His brother Leopold, in turn, who succeeded after a few years, reverted to the earlier policy of his mother, and resolutely opposed the further dismemberment of Poland. Francis, who followed his father, after another short reign of two years, though very young and inexperienced, was hardly in the saddle before he effected another complete *volte face* in the foreign affairs of his Empire. He threw himself into the arms of the Empress Catherine in the hope of sharing with her in the spoil of Poland. He was completely outwitted by that astute woman in the second partition. This only made him the more greedy to join in the third and last partition. Having decided to abandon the ancient ally of his House, there were no limits to his perfidies in pursuit of his object. There was little difference in this respect between Francis and Frederick William. Indeed, the two monarchs closely resembled one another. Both were equally without capacity as generals and statesmen. Both distrusted themselves and the experienced officials who advised their predecessors. Both fell under the influence of unscrupulous adventurers, such as Lucchesini and Thugut. Both were entirely devoid of moral principles in their relations to other Powers. It is not a pleasant reflection that, in spite of their disqualifications, the two monarchs attained the object of their ambition mainly by the aid of Russia, and largely aggrandized their domains by the plunder of an unoffending neighbour. Up to the present time there has been no reversal of these misdeeds. The Poles remain under subjection to their foes. But 150 years form only a short period in the history of a nation. The resuscitation of the smaller nationalities, in the south-east of Europe, was effected after more than 500 years of subjection to a foreign and barbarous Empire. It is difficult to believe that twenty millions of Poles will not, sooner or later, achieve a complete corporate existence, if not independence.

Meanwhile it may well be doubted whether, even from the narrow point of view of expediency and self-interest, the two Powers, Prussia and Austria, acted wisely in destroying the buffer State which lay between them and Russia. The time has not yet arrived for forming a final judgment on this. But we may affirm that, at the bar of history, the destruction of the Polish Kingdom, and the partition of its territory, were political crimes of the gravest kind, unequalled in the past of Europe. In apportioning the blame for it, we are justified in the conclusion, that the conduct of Prussia was the most perfidious and mendacious, that of Russia the most cunning and deadly, and that of Austria the most mean and treacherous.

CHAPTER XIII

NAPOLEON AND THE DUCHY OF WARSAW

THE Empress Catherine died in 1796, within a few months of having practically achieved one of the two main objects of her ambitious career, in the extinction of the Kingdom of Poland, and the incorporation of nearly two-thirds of its territory as Russian provinces.* She was succeeded by her son, the Emperor Paul, who was animated by most friendly sympathy for the Poles, though he was not prepared to undo the work of his mother. He personally visited Kosciuszko in prison, embraced him, gave him his freedom, and made offers of employment in the Russian service, and of large grants of money, which the patriotic General refused. He also released the numerous Poles who had been imprisoned by Catherine. Twelve

* The final treaty between the three Powers was not signed till 1797, but the terms of it were virtually agreed to in Catherine's lifetime.

thousand of them, who had been deported to Siberia, were allowed to return to Poland. Prussia for a time also adopted a policy of clemency, while Austria maintained its severe régime of repression in Galicia.

The Poles, however, were not appeased by the tardy clemency of the two Powers, or deterred by the harsh measures of the third. They still nursed hopes of recovering their independence. They formed expectations of assistance from the Republican Government of France. They offered to raise a Polish legion to assist in the war against Austria. The Directory at Paris were unable to accept the offer, as the law of France, at that time, forbade the employment of foreign troops. But when a Provisional Government was formed by the Italians in Lombardy, it was arranged with them that a Polish legion should be taken into their service, though virtually they were under the orders of the local French Generals. Five thousand Poles were enlisted for this purpose. They fought side by side with the French in many a hard battle in Italy against the Austrians.

When, in 1799, Napoleon was raised to the Consulate of France, the law forbidding the employment of foreign troops was repealed by the new Constitution, and the Polish legion was taken directly under the pay and service of France. It was greatly increased in numbers. There must have been a continuous stream of recruits from Poland, for the losses of the Legion were very great. It was always in the thick of the war. In 1801, when peace was made between France and Austria, by the Treaty of Lunéville, the corps consisted of 15,000. Its end was tragic. It was sent as part of a large army, under General Leclerc, the brother-in-law of Napoleon, to St. Domingo, in the West Indies, where it was employed in vain efforts to put down the rebellion of the negroes, under Toussaint l'Ouverture, a leader not less patriotic and noble than Kosciuszko. It shared the fate of Leclerc and his army, and perished from yellow fever. Very few, if any, of them ever returned to Europe. It was believed in some quarters that Napoleon was not sorry to be rid of the Polish legion and of his brother-in-law, and sent them to the West Indies with that object.

In 1806, when war broke out between France and Prussia, there seemed to be hope again for the Poles. Napoleon held out vague expectations to them. A new Polish legion was raised. Kosciuszko, who had been living in exile at Fontainebleau, since his release from prison in Russia, refused to join in a movement in Poland in favour of Napoleon. "What! Despotism for despotism!" he said. "The Poles have enough of it at home, without going so far to purchase it at the price of their blood."

After the battle of Jena, on October 14, 1806, which destroyed the military power of Prussia, the French army under Napoleon threatened Prussian Poland. Without waiting for its arrival, the Poles broke out in insurrection, and with the aid of 15,000 men from Lithuania, drove the Prussians from Kalisz and other fortified places. Napoleon entered Posen on November 17th, and was received with enthusiasm by the Poles of that province. He issued a vague and enigmatical proclamation:—

> "Shall the throne of Poland be re-established, and shall this great nation resume its existence and independence? Shall it spring from the abyss of the tomb to life again? God only, who holds in His hands the issues of all events, is the Arbiter of this great political problem; but certainly there never was a more memorable or a more interesting event."

The manifesto was not inspiring or convincing. It would seem that Napoleon was without any policy for Poland, and played fast and loose with the question of its independence, as suited him from time to time. For the moment he seemed disposed to favour this. His army entered Warsaw on January 14, 1807, after the battle of Pultusk, and Prussian Poland was cleared of Russian and Prussian troops.

A provisional Government was then formed at Warsaw, for those parts of Poland which had been allotted to Prussia, in 1793 and 1795. A little later war broke out between Russia and France. It was expected that Napoleon would take the opportunity of proclaiming the reconstitution of the old Kingdom of Poland, and would appeal for the patriotic support of the Poles. He did not avail himself of the opportunity. He did not apparently wish for war *à outrance* with Russia. After the defeat of Russia at the battle of Friedland on June 14, 1807, peace was made; and the Treaty of Tilsit was signed between France, Russia, and Prussia. It secured independence for the Prussian part of Poland, including the provinces of Posen and Warsaw, but not of West Prussia. The title of Grand Duchy of Warsaw was given to it. It had a population of about three millions. The King of Saxony was, in future, to be Grand Duke of this province. A new Constitution of a very liberal character was promulgated by Napoleon. Serfdom was to be abolished. The King of Saxony took possession of this duchy on November 16th, and appointed a Ministry wholly of native Poles, who were to be responsible to the Diet. Prince Poniatowski was placed at the head of the army. A Polish Diet met in March 1809. It introduced the Code Napoléon into the new province by a large majority.

In 1809 war was again declared between Austria and France. The Archduke Frederick, with 30,000 Austrians, invaded the duchy of Warsaw, and after a fierce battle with the Polish army occupied the capital. Poniatowski then boldly, and with great skill, marched with his small army into Galicia, raised the standard of revolt there against the Austrians, and was supported by the whole population. As a result, the Archduke was compelled to evacuate Warsaw, and to retreat with his army to Austria. Poniatowski obtained command of the whole of Galicia, and, with the approval of Napoleon, appointed a provisional Government there.

Meanwhile, Napoleon had invaded Austria,

and, on July 6th, defeated its army at Wagram. By the Treaty of Vienna which followed, four departments of Galicia, including Cracow and Sandomir, were added to the duchy of Warsaw, and two were handed over to Russia, while the valuable salt-mines of Wieliczka were to be held in common by Austria and the Duchy.

The Duchy, therefore, was extended by the addition of about two-thirds of Galicia. Russia not only remained in possession of what it had acquired in previous partitions, but obtained extension from Austria. This arrangement of a very ephemeral character may be considered as a repartition of the unfortunate Poland. It lasted for only five years. During this time the Duchy of Warsaw had a nominal independence. Practically it was a dependency of France, in the leading-strings of the French Ambassador, and with its army under the command of Napoleon, but otherwise enjoying an autonomy. The population seems to have been thoroughly exhausted by the efforts of the previous few years. De Pradt, the French Ambassador, says of it in his Memoirs: "Nothing could exceed the misery of all classes. The army was not paid. The officers were in rags. The best houses in Warsaw were in ruins. The greatest lords were compelled to leave Warsaw for the want of money to provide their tables."

The Poles, however, submitted to the enormous military expenditure imposed on them by Napoleon, in the hope that there would soon be an extension of their country to its old limits. There seemed to be very good prospect of this in 1812, when Napoleon, again at war with Russia, entered upon his great invasion of that country. With a view to the full support of the Poles, he gave out that he intended to restore to Poland its former territory. Marshal Duroc was directed to remove any impressions to the contrary, and to give an assurance to the Poles of the Emperor's interest in their cause. But there was every reason to believe that he was not in earnest. He made no proclamation to the people of Prussian Poland, or of Lithuania, when his army entered these districts. He made a secret treaty with the Emperor of Austria, undertaking to cede Galicia to him in exchange for some Illyrian province. The Emperor of Russia (Alexander) met the intrigues of Napoleon with the Poles by promises of autonomy to Lithuania.

On the other hand, on June 20th, a meeting of the Diet of the duchy of Warsaw was opened with a speech prepared by the French Ambassador, under the express instructions of Napoleon, in which language was used as to a Kingdom of Poland, which roused the enthusiasm of the Poles at Warsaw and elsewhere. The Polish army had been largely increased, and no fewer than 80,000 of its men, under the command of Poniatowski, joined the Grande Armée which invaded Russia.

The army entered Lithuania, and reached Wilna, its capital, on June 9th. A deputation from its Diet met Napoleon, and presented an address to him which he had dictated himself, and to which he replied in the following ambiguous terms:—

"In my situation I have many interests to conciliate and many duties to perform. If I had reigned at the time of the first, second, or third partitions of Poland, I would have armed all my people to support you. . . . I love your nation. During the last sixteen years I have seen your soldiers at my side in the fields of Italy, as well as those of Spain. I applaud all that you have done; I sanction the efforts you wish to make; I will do everything in my power to second your resolutions. . . . I have always used the same language since my first appearance in Poland. I must add here that I have guaranteed Austria the integrity of her States, and that I cannot authorize any design or step that may tend to disturb her in the peaceable possession of the Polish provinces which remain under her power. Let

Lithuania, Samogitia, Witepsk, Polock, Mohilow, Wolhynia, the Ukraine, and Podolia be animated with the same spirit which I have witnessed in Great Poland, and Providence will crown with success the purity of your cause, and will reward this devotion to your country, which has so much interested me in your behalf, and has given you so many claims to my esteem and protection, on which you may depend under all circumstances."

The reply of the Emperor was held to be evasive. It roused no enthusiasm in Lithuania. An appeal for men to join the army and to march against Russia, met with no response. In an address to his army on entering the province, the Emperor spoke of it as an enemy's country. The soldiers acted on this suggestion. The route of the army was marked by devastation and ruin. Villages were burnt, men were murdered, women were ravished.

The Polish troops, under Prince Poniatowski, formed the fifth corps of the Grande Armée. They distinguished themselves greatly at Smolensk, Borodino, Kalouga, and other battles. They shared in all the horrors of the retreat. Of the 80,000, not more than 3,000 survived in the ranks, when they finally reached Cracow in company with the remnant of the Austrian army. After the abandonment of Warsaw the National Government collapsed. Its members dispersed. The Russians took possession of the city and province without opposition. In spite of these disasters, Poniatowski, at Cracow, raised a fresh force of 15,000 Poles, of whom 5,000 were cavalry, and they joined Napoleon in Saxony, for his disastrous campaign of 1813. They formed the eighth corps of his army, and took part in the battles of Dresden and Leipzig. At the latter, Poniatowski was ordered to defend the retreat of the main army after their defeat. The bridge over the River Elster was blown up prematurely before the rearguard of Poles had crossed. Many of them endeavoured to escape by swimming across the river. Poniatowski, who, four days before, had been made a Marshal of France, as a reward for his great services in command of his corps, plunged into the river and was drowned. It is said that he courted death in this way, rather than survive the disastrous defeat, and that he exclaimed: "God has given the honour of the Poles into my keeping, and only unto God will I give it up." The few survivors of the Polish army followed Napoleon, and fought for him at the battle of Hanau on October 30, 1813. They accompanied Napoleon to Paris in 1814, and we hear of some of them again fighting for him in the campaign in France of that year, and again in his last and final reverse at Waterloo in 1815.

Meanwhile, the Russians had occupied the whole of Poland, including both Galicia and Posen. Kosciuszko, on April 9, 1814, made an appeal to the Emperor Alexander on behalf of the Poles :—

"I request three favours of you : the first is to grant a general amnesty to the Poles without any restriction, and that the serfs scattered in foreign countries may be regarded as free if they return to their homes ; the second, that your Majesty will proclaim yourself king of Poland, with a free Constitution approaching that of England, and that you cause schools to be established there for the instruction of the serfs ; that their servitude be abolished at the end of ten years, and that they may enjoy the full possession of their property. If my prayers are granted, I will go in person (though ill) to throw myself at your Majesty's feet to thank you, and to be the first to render homage to my sovereign." *

The Emperor, in an autographic letter, replied :—

"I feel great satisfaction, General, in answering your letter. Your wishes shall be accomplished. With the help of the Almighty, I trust to realize the regeneration of the brave and respectable nation to which you belong. I have made a solemn engagement, and its welfare has always occupied my thoughts. . . . How satisfactory it

* *Mémoires d'Oginski*, vol. iv. p. 175.

would be to me, General, to see you my helpmate in the accomplishment of these salutary labours! Your name, your character, your talents, will be my best support."

It will be seen that the Emperor later did his best to act up to the spirit of this letter. The Poles of the Grande Armée were allowed to return to Poland in company with the Russian army. They were placed under the command of the Grand Duke Constantine. On their return to Poland they were allowed the option either to remain in the service of Russia, or to retire.

The Emperor on his return to St. Petersburg, in July 1814, received a deputation from Lithuania, and in the course of his reply said: "Tell your constituents that all is forgotten and pardoned, and that they must not have any doubt of the interest that I feel for them and the desire I have to see them happy and content."

CHAPTER XIV

REPARTITION BY THE CONGRESS OF VIENNA

After the conclusion of the war, in 1814, the abdication of Napoleon, and his departure to Elba, a Congress of the European Powers was held at Vienna. Its members met in September for the purpose of settling the future map of Europe. The Poles were not represented directly there. Strange to say, their claim for reconstitution as a nation was presented to the Congress by the Emperor Alexander of Russia. He was an idealist, as some of his predecessors and descendants have been. He was far ahead of all other members of the Congress in popular instincts and almost democratic tendencies. He had great sympathy for the Poles, and had pledged his word to them. He had by his side, as adviser, Prince Adam Czartoryski, the most distinguished Pole of the time, and his life-long personal friend.

Alexander dominated the Congress by his great

personality. He was also in a very strong position there, for his army was in actual possession of the whole of the Duchy of Warsaw, and also of Saxony. The Emperor Francis dispensed a splendid hospitality to the other monarchs and statesmen, but he wisely left the negotiations in the hands of Prince Metternich, a most astute statesman, a worthy successor of Kaunitz and Thugut in crooked diplomacy and reactionary politics. England and France were represented respectively by Lord Castlereagh and Prince Talleyrand. It may be well, in explanation of the part taken by Castlereagh on the Polish question, which alone concerns us, to quote from a memorandum drawn up for his guidance by Lord Liverpool on behalf of the British Government.

"There can be no doubt that the restoration of the Kingdom of Poland, such as it was in the year 1792, under an hereditary, independent, and limited monarchy, would be the measure most just in itself and most satisfactory to the people of this country.

"Have we any right, however, to call upon Russia, Austria, and Prussia to give up those provinces of Poland which they have annexed to their own dominions, and which continue to form a part of them? Certainly not. We may recommend it, but we can do no more. For however unjust the partition of Poland may have been, if from considerations of prudence we either found it impracticable, or did not deem it expedient to oppose them at the time they were made, we can have no right at the distance of five, ten, or twenty years, to require of the above named Powers to dismember the provinces which they then annexed, and which formed part of their dominions during a period in which we were at peace with all of them and in alliance with some of them.

The only portion, therefore, of ancient Poland about whose fate we have now a right to take a decisive part is the Duchy of Warsaw. The fate of that Duchy is *sub judice.*

It is obvious that an arrangement may be made with respect to the Duchy of Warsaw upon either of the three following principles :—

1. It may be divided between the three great Powers, and so made to constitute a part of each of their dominions.

2. It may be preserved as an independent State under an independent prince.

3. It may be assigned to one of the three great Powers as an independent State, which under the present circumstances must be Russia. *

The memorandum then proceeded to discuss in detail these three methods, and concluded by expressing the opinion that the third of them was most to the interest of Europe.

It soon appeared at the Congress that the independence of Poland, or even of the Duchy of Warsaw, was out of the question. The Emperor Alexander would not listen to any such proposal. Putting his hand on the map of Poland, he is reported to have said, " C'est à moi." He seemed

* The memorandum is printed at length in the Life of Lord Liverpool, ii. p. 37.

to be specially incensed against Austria. "Je donnerai," he said, "ce qu'il faut à la Prusse, mais je ne donnerai pas une village à l'Autriche. J'ai conquis le Duché et j'ai 480,000 hommes à le garder." He insisted that the dismembered parts of Poland, as it was before 1793, should be reunited, and should form a kingdom, under the suzerainty of the Emperor of Russia, with complete autonomy. Poland thus reconstituted was to include the province of Lithuania. This wide scheme was very unpopular with his Russian Ministers, but Alexander insisted on it. The scheme, so far as it proposed to include in the Kingdom of Poland, all the parts which Austria and Prussia had acquired in the partitions of 1772 and 1793-5, was strongly opposed by those Powers, backed up by England. Talleyrand also opposed on behalf of France, mainly with the object of sowing discord and distrust in the Congress.

Alexander succeeded in obtaining the support of Prussia by promising to compensate it for the loss of its Polish provinces, by the annexation of the whole of Saxony. This added to the indignation and opposition of Austria, who had no wish to see Prussia aggrandized in Germany. It raised vehement opposition from the smaller

States of Germany. With the object of forcing the hands of the Congress, Alexander gave orders to Prince Repnin, who was in command of the Russian troops in Saxony, to hand over that kingdom to Prussia, and to march to Warsaw and proclaim himself (the Tsar) as King of Poland, with the promise of a complete autonomous Constitution. In other words, he proposed to carry out, by arrangement with Prussia, and behind the backs of the other Powers, the scheme which he had submitted in vain to the Congress. When this intention became known, it caused the greatest indignation and discontent among other members of the Congress. There followed a combination, and a secret treaty between the other Powers, with the exception of Prussia, against Russia. The Congress was on the point of being dissolved, and war would undoubtedly have broken out between Russia and some of the other Powers. At the last moment, however, more prudent counsels prevailed. By great pressure the Emperor Alexander was induced to reduce his full demand for the reconstitution of the old Kingdom of Poland. It was found that Prussia would be content with a part of Saxony, if some portion of her original Polish provinces was restored to her.

An ingenious scheme, devised by Metternich by way of compromise, was eventually agreed to by the other Powers. It amounted to a new partition of Poland. Alexander's very generous intentions to the Poles were in great part set aside. Galicia was restored to Austria, with the exception of the city of Cracow, and its surrounding district, which was constituted as an independent republic, guaranteed by the Great Powers. The Polish province of Posen, together with the cities of Danzig and Thorn, were given again to Prussia, who was content with about a third of Saxony, in place of the parts of Poland which she had acquired in 1795, including the city of Warsaw. The residue of the Grand Duchy of Warsaw was placed under the suzerainty of Russia, with the promise of autonomous institutions, in accord with the proposal of the Emperor. It included Warsaw and the districts taken from Prussia. Russia also retained Lithuania and the other Slav provinces of the old Kingdom of Poland. It is unnecessary to advert, save in the briefest way, to the other territorial arrangements of the Congress. Prussia regained its provinces on the left of the Rhine. France was restricted to her boundaries as they were before 1792, retaining, however, Alsace and

Lorraine. Belgium was not restored to Austria, but was united to the Kingdom of Holland. Austria was confirmed in its ownership of Lombardy and Venetia. Norway was not restored to Denmark, but was retained by Sweden. Great Britain retained Malta and Heligoland; and the Ionian Islands were placed under her protection. She also retained, but not under the Treaty of Vienna, most of the colonies captured during the war from France, Holland, and Spain.

The compromise between the Great Powers on the subject of Poland was arrived at on February 11, 1815. Four days later Castlereagh left Vienna and returned to London, where his presence was urgently needed by his colleagues for discussions in the House of Commons. He was replaced at the Congress by the Duke of Wellington. On February 25th Napoleon escaped from Elba, and his first words on landing in France were "Le Congrès est dissous." The wish was father to the thought, but was not realized in the sense he desired. The news of his escape reached Vienna on March 4th. It had the effect of inducing the Congress to come to an immediate decision on the few questions of importance remaining unsettled. Its leading members then hastily dispersed, many of them to take part against the common enemy in the war, which ended a few weeks later on the field of Waterloo.

The actual Treaty of Vienna, embodying the conclusions of the Congress, was signed before the great battle, on June 11th. Its main provisions, however, were made known to the public at a much earlier date, for on March 20th Castlereagh, in the House of Commons, explained and defended them in a long and laboured speech. On the subject of Poland, he made a great point of the provision in the treaty by which autonomous institutions were secured to the Poles, under the three Powers who divided their territory.

> "The main object," he said, "of conciliating the Poles would not be lost sight of. They would be relieved from the local difficulties and personal disqualifications under which they had hitherto laboured. Whatever system of policy might have formerly existed, the Poles would now be governed as Poles." *

On this point the words of the treaty were these:—

> "The Poles who are respectively subjects of Russia, Austria, and Prussia shall obtain a Representation and

* *Parliamentary History*, March 20, 1815.

National Constitution regulated according to the degree of political consideration that each Government to which they belong shall judge expedient and proper to give to them."

As regards the Duchy of Warsaw, the article incorporating it as a kingdom under the suzerainty of the Tzar was as follows:—

"The Duchy of Warsaw, with the exception of the provinces which are otherwise disposed of, is united to the Russian Empire. It shall be irrevocably attached to it by its Constitution, and be possessed by His Majesty the Emperor of all the Russias, his heirs and successors in perpetuity. His Imperial Majesty reserves to himself to give to this State enjoying a distinct administration the interior improvements which he shall think proper. He shall assume with his other titles that of Tzar, King of Poland."

Nothing was said in the treaty as to autonomy for Lithuanians and others of the ancient Slav provinces of the Kingdom of Poland. Although the generous intentions of Alexander for reconstituting the whole of Great Poland, by uniting again to it the parts made over to Austria and Prussia, were not agreed to, and a new and last partition was effected, yet so much of his scheme as involved a Kingdom of Poland, under the tutelage of Russia, with autonomous institutions, was provided for, and was sanctioned by the treaty.

The Emperor Alexander, before leaving Vienna, announced the decision of the Congress to the people of Poland in a letter to the Polish Senate at Warsaw.

"The Kingdom of Poland," he said, "will be united with Russia by the bond of its own Constitution. If the great interests of general tranquillity have not permitted the union of all the Poles under the same sceptre, I have at least endeavoured to alleviate as much as possible the pain of separation, and to obtain for them everywhere the peaceful enjoyment of their nationality."

It is clear that, in the view of the Emperor, the arrangements of the Congress of Vienna in favour of some form of autonomy to the parts of Poland ceded to the three Powers were of a valid and permanent character, invested with the sanction of the other Powers of Europe.

The King of Prussia was evidently of the same opinion, for, in a proclamation of May 15, 1815, issued to the people of the province of Posen on his resuming possession of it, he said :—

"Inhabitants of the Grand Duchy of Posen, you are incorporated with my monarchy, but without being obliged to renounce your nationality. You will participate in the Constitution which I intend to give to my faithful subjects, and you will have a provincial Constitution like the other provinces of my kingdom. Your religion shall be maintained. Your personal rights and your property shall remain under the protection of the laws upon which you will also be called upon in future to deliberate. Your language shall be used with the German in all public transactions, and every one of you, according to his abilities, shall be eligible to public employment in the Grand Duchy and to all the offices and dignities in my kingdom."

It is clear, therefore, from these manifestoes that both Russia and Prussia were prepared to give effect to the provisions of the Treaty of Vienna in favour of autonomy for their Polish provinces.

CHAPTER XV

THE POLES UNDER THREE MASTERS

A HUNDRED years have elapsed since the Treaty of Vienna, in 1815, which settled the final reparti-tion of Poland between its three neighbouring Powers. It will be well, in conclusion, to describe briefly what they have respectively done with their shares of the plunder, and how they have performed the trust confided to them by the Congress.

There can be no doubt whatever that the Emperor Alexander most honestly and earnestly desired to restore and maintain the national exist-ence of the Poles, and to endow them with an autonomous representative Constitution, under the protection of Russia. Indeed, from his subsequent language to the Polish Diet, it appears that he intended to include Lithuania and the Ukraine within their kingdom, and also to extend autonomous constitutions to other parts of his Empire, if the experiment in Poland should prove to be successful. If his demands had been acceded to by the Congress, Poland would not have been partitioned between the three Powers. Its nationality would have been maintained under the supremacy of Russia, and many of the subsequent troubles might have been avoided.

Unfortunately, the Emperor made the initial mistake of appointing his brother, the Grand Duke Constantine, as Commander-in-Chief of the army in Poland, and General Zaionezsk, a native Pole, as Viceroy. The latter was a nonentity, who fell completely under the influence of the Grand Duke. Constantine was a reactionary imbued with the principles of the old Russian party, with an overbearing temper, capricious and headstrong, and without a spark of his brother's liberal tendencies, and sympathy for the Poles. He was a military martinet, a glorified drill-sergeant, the author of the *mot* that "wars are hateful because they spoil armies." He persuaded the Emperor, on this account, not to employ the Polish army in the war against Turkey. The old Russian party was also represented by Novosiltsoff, a reactionary Russian, who held an anomalous position as a member of the Council, and urged the Grand Duke to arbitrary measures against the Poles. He was regarded as the evil spirit of Poland.

Alexander paid his first visit to Poland in November, 1815, and was received with the greatest enthusiasm. His efforts for the Polish cause at the Congress of Vienna were well known to the people of Warsaw, and sanguine hopes were raised as to the future. At his instance a new Constitution was drawn up for the Kingdom of Poland by Prince Adam Czartoryski. It was on the lines of that of 1791, but was distinctly more advanced. It was of the most liberal character. If adhered to it would have amply secured self-government to the Poles in the new kingdom, as regards internal affairs. The Diet was formed of two Chambers, the one of members nominated for life by the Emperor, the other of representatives, one half elected by the class of nobles, the other by burghers and other classes of the community. It was to meet every second year. No taxes could be imposed without its consent. The action of Ministers was subject to its approval. The Polish language was alone to be used. Personal liberty was secured. No person could be arrested and imprisoned otherwise than by legal process. Freedom of the Press and religious toleration were assured. The army, consisting of 20,000 infantry and 6,000 cavalry, was to be a national one, under the command of a General appointed by the Tsar. The Viceroy was to be either a member of the royal family of Romanoff or a Pole. All appointments, civil and military, were reserved for Poles. The Emperor of Russia was in future to be crowned as King of Poland, and was to take a solemn oath to maintain the Constitution. Foreign affairs alone were reserved for the Russian Government. There were few Constitutions in Europe at the time so liberal. Many persons, however, disbelieved in its maintenance. It seemed unlikely that the Russians would tolerate such popular institutions for Poland, a subject country, when they themselves were governed by a severe autocracy. Kosciuszko, when consulted about it, wrote to Prince Czartoryski: "From the first I foresee a very different state of things. The Russians will occupy equally with us the chief places of government. This certainly will not inspire the Poles with any great confidence. They foresee, not without fear, that in time the Polish name will fall into contempt, and that the Russians will soon treat us as their own subjects." * It will be seen that his fears were fully justified.

The Emperor Alexander gave his formal sanction to the Constitution, and in 1818 opened the first meeting of the Diet. "Your hopes and mine," he said in his speech, "are being realized. You have given me the opportunity of disclosing to my own country that which I have been long preparing for it, and which it will obtain as soon as you have proved yourselves equal to your task. The result of your labours will teach me whether, true to my undertaking, I shall be able to extend what I have already done for you."

He also held out hopes that part of Lithuania would be added to the kingdom of Poland.† The Diet justified its existence by passing several measures of utility. Alexander closed its session in person by a speech from the throne, in which he said, "I abide by the execution of my intentions. What they are you know well."

The good intentions of the Emperor, however,

* Fletcher, p. 391.

† The Emperor included in the new Kingdom of Poland, not only the parts of the Duchy of Warsaw ceded to it by the Treaty of Vienna, but also the purely Polish districts outside the Duchy which had been annexed by the Empress Catherine in 1795.

were nullified by his brother Constantine, who had no sympathy with, or understanding of, a Constitutional Government. His instincts were those of an autocrat. If an article appeared in a newspaper which displeased him, he sent a file of soldiers to break up the type, and to suppress the paper. Conflicts very early arose between him and the Diet. Any member of the Diet who opposed or criticized the policy of the Government was arrested and sent to prison. The University of Warsaw was suppressed because some of its students gave vent to Liberal opinions. The second Diet refused to pass some of his measures, and impeached the Ministers. The Grand Duke replied by neglecting to summon another Diet for five years, between 1820 and 1825. During this time Poland was subjected to a continually increasing rigour of arbitrary rule.

A third Diet met in 1825, but the publication of its debates was forbidden. The Emperor, on opening this Diet, addressed it in frigid and warning terms. He had, in the interval, lost most of his enthusiasm for Liberal principles, and had fallen under the influence of the old Russian party. The Diet, however, gave its consent to all the measures submitted to it, and apparently Alexander was appeased, for, in closing its session, he said: "You have carried out the expectations of the Government. It will be my earnest desire to convince you what an influence your action will have in the future."

These were the last words of Alexander to the Poles. He died within a few weeks, and was succeeded, not by the Grand Duke Constantine, the next in line of succession, who was recognized by every one, including himself, as quite unfit to occupy the throne of Russia, and who voluntarily, during Alexander's lifetime, agreed to be excluded from the succession, but by his youngest brother. Nicholas, eighteen years younger than Alexander, was of a very different stamp—a true autocrat without any popular sympathies. He was crowned at Warsaw as King of Poland, and solemnly took the oath in public, as prescribed by law, to maintain the Constitution which had been granted by his brother.

Having gone through this ceremony, Nicholas proceeded to sanction every measure proposed to him by reactionary advisers for setting aside the Constitution. Arbitrary arrests were multiplied. Freedom of the Press was abolished. Russians were appointed to posts in the civil and military service. Taxes were levied without the consent of the Diet. Monopolies were created, and the proceeds were squandered by the Government. Councils of War were authorized to supersede the civil law. The responsibility of Ministers to the Diet was set aside. Five years were allowed to elapse since the last Diet before the next was summoned. Practically the system of autocratic Government in Russia was extended to Poland.

As a result of all these infractions of the Constitution, discontent spread throughout Poland. Secret societies multipled in all directions. On November 29, 1830, in sympathy apparently with the revolution in France, a popular outbreak occurred at Warsaw. The Polish army took part with the people. The Grand Duke lost his head. He fled from the capital with the Russian troops in garrison there, abandoning the Citadel, and its great store of arms and ammunition. The whole country was soon in open rebellion. The Polish army was put under the command of General Chlopicki, a surviving veteran of Napoleon's army. The Diet was summoned. It endeavoured to open negotiations with the Russian Government, on the basis of a full recognition and maintenance of the

Constitution. Nicholas refused to parley with insurgents. The Diet then proceeded to decree the deposition of the Romanoffs and the establishment of a republic. There was a striking resemblance between the present proceedings at Warsaw, and what had taken place in the outbreak, in 1794, above described. There was the same division of opinion among its people, the same contention of factions. The moderate party, consisting of the larger landowners and wealthier people, having little hope of ultimate success against the great forces of Russia, were unwilling to proceed to extremities, though sympathizing with the national cause. They endeavoured to restrain the ardour of the extreme party, and to base the movement on the Treaty of Vienna. The republican party, on the other hand, would admit of no negotiation. They were the more numerous, and gave its main force to the movement. There was a violent popular outbreak, which resulted in the hanging of some of the suspected moderates. In spite of these conflicts of factions, the Poles fought for their cause with desperation and heroism. General Chlopicki resigned, and Prince Radzivill was put in command of the army.

The Diet appealed to the Powers of Europe for

assistance, and issued a manifesto setting forth, in strong language, the wrongs of Poland. They showed that the Treaty of Vienna had been set aside by Russia, and that the Poles were consequently entitled to a restoration of their independence. The Governments of England and France declined to intervene on their behalf by force. They contented themselves with a mild protest to the Russian Court, pointing out the infraction of the Treaty of Vienna. The reply of the Russian Court was that the obligations of the Treaty of Vienna were reciprocal, and that the Poles, by declaring their independence, had lost their right to claim the maintenance of the Constitution, under the terms of the treaty. The Emperor resented the intervention of other Powers. The Polish Diet refrained from calling on the Poles in Galicia and Prussian Poland to join in the movement, for they did not wish to have both Austria and Prussia ranged in arms against them.

In the meantime, the Emperor Nicholas was not slow to answer the challenge of the Poles. Early in 1831 he sent an army of 120,000 into Poland, under Marshal Diebitsch. The Poles made an heroic defence. They were successful in some of the earlier encounters with detached columns of the Russians, but they were ultimately overpowered by numbers. The peasantry of Poland and Lithuania do not appear to have taken so much part as in the outbreak of 1794. We do not read of their coming into the field armed with scythe-blades. The insurgents were mainly from the *petite noblesse* and from the townspeople. The main Polish army, under General Skrzynecki, met with a crushing defeat on May 26th at Ostrolenka. Shortly after this, Marshal Diebitsch and the Grand Duke Constantine, who accompanied him, succumbed to cholera. The former was replaced by Marshal Paskievich, who showed great energy and determination. On September 8th, the lines in front of Warsaw were successfully stormed. The city then capitulated. By the end of November, the insurrection was put down, and the country was cleared of the insurgent bands. The Russian Government had the full sympathy of Prussia in crushing the Polish rebellion. "Poland," said the Prussian Minister, "had better be annihilated, so as to have done with her once for all."

Nicholas followed up his success with ruthless and relentless vigour and cruelty. He issued a manifesto, offering what he called an amnesty, but which excepted every one who, directly or indirectly, was concerned in the outbreak. In 1832 the Constitution accorded by Alexander was formally annulled. The Diet was abolished. The Polish language was proscribed. The Government departments in Poland were made branches of the Civil Service in Russia, and received their orders from St. Petersburg. The Polish army was merged in that of Russia. Russians were appointed to all posts of any importance, civil and military. The Russian system was introduced into the Polish tribunals. A strict censorship of the Press was established. Arbitrary arrests became the usual order of the day. Everything was done to suppress the Roman Catholic Church. Their convents were closed. Their property was secularized. The Polish language was forbidden in the churches. The schools, such as existed, ceased to be Polish. The instruction was to be in the Russian language. Russification was enforced in every possible way.

The Ukase of February 26, 1832, by which most of these changes were effected, was intended to remove Poland from the list of nations, so far as Russia could effect this. The use of the national flag of Poland was prohibited. A beginning was even made of removing the population. Forty-five thousand families were transplanted from Poland to the Caucasus and the district of the Don. Polish orphans were drafted to military colonies. In thousands of cases banishment and confiscation of property were awarded. When the confiscated properties were put up for sale Russians alone were permitted to bid for them. Polish refugees spread over Europe. Sentences of death were recorded against them in their absence.

The same harsh measures were adopted in Lithuania, where there had also been an outbreak in sympathy with that in Poland. General Mouravieff, in command of the Russian forces there, put it down with the utmost ferocity. Many thousands were deported to Siberia. Mouravieff even prepared to remove the whole population. But this part of his programme was not approved by the Emperor.

Thenceforth, until after the death of the Emperor Nicholas, which occurred during the Crimean War in 1855, there was no alleviation of the régime of severity and terror. His successor, Alexander II, showed a disposition towards more lenient treatment of the Poles. In 1861, at the instance of the Marquis

Vielopolski, the most eminent Pole of his time, the Emperor made some important concessions to the Poles. A separate Ministry was created in Poland for education and religion, with Vielopolski at its head, and with the intention apparently of reversing or modifying the proscription of the Polish language. Elective local councils were to be appointed, with power to appeal to the central Government.

It appeared from statements made later by Prince Gortchakoff to the British Ambassador at St. Petersburg, Lord Napier, that it was the intention of the Emperor to carry this policy still further, and to give to Poland a certain measure of autonomy, with due consideration for their language and religion. But the Emperor in a public speech at Warsaw warned the Poles against indulging in dreams. His reforms and promises came too late. Already Poland was seething with disaffection and discontent. Secret societies again multiplied in the towns. At Warsaw a secret revolutionary tribunal was established, which issued decrees, and directed the assassination of obnoxious Russians. Another outbreak became imminent. It was precipitated, in 1863, by the Russian Government, under a law authorizing conscription for the army, making a sudden swoop by night on all the young men whom they suspected of disaffection, 2,000 in number, and sending them as conscripts to the military depots in Siberia and the Caucasus. This had the effect, which was doubtless intended by the old Russian party, of lashing the Poles into frenzy and revolt. There followed a confused and general *mêlée* of insurrection throughout the country. It was a hopeless movement from the very first. There was no longer a Polish army to act as a nucleus of armed resistance. To wage war with undisciplined bands against the whole power of Russia was an act of madness.

The only real hope of the insurgents was the intervention of foreign Powers. There was much sympathy for the Polish cause in Western Europe, especially in England and France. In 1863 there were debates on the subject in both Houses of Parliament in England. There was unanimity there that the treatment of the Poles was in direct violation of the Treaty of Vienna. In response to public opinion the Government of Lord Palmerston made a remonstrance to the Russian Government, appealing to the treaty. There ensued a diplomatic correspondence of importance and interest. The Russian

Government, in the first instance, through Prince Gortchakoff, replied in conciliatory terms. He pointed out that the Poles themselves were not relying on the Treaty of Vienna, and were not asking for amelioration of their treatment. They would be satisfied with nothing less than their independence. They had taken up arms to assert it. They also insisted on the incorporation with Poland of Lithuania and other Russian provinces. The Prince claimed that Russia no longer held Poland by virtue of the Treaty of Vienna, but by right of conquest, effected at the time of the rebellion of 1831. All the same, he said, the Russian Government was not unwilling to enter on an exchange of ideas upon the ground, and within the limits, of the Treaty of Vienna.

Lord Russell, the Foreign Minister in England, maintained, in reply, that it was the deliberate intention of the Emperor Alexander I, and the other members of the Congress of Vienna, that Poland should be endowed with a national administration, congenial to the sentiments of the people; that the Emperor in 1815 granted to Poland a Constitution conformable to these intentions, but that religious liberty and political freedom had since been abrogated by the

Russian Government, and had only been partially renewed under the recent changes. He directed attention to the following points:—

(1) That a complete amnesty should be accorded to all concerned in the outbreak. (2) That national representation should be given to Poland. (3) That Poles should be appointed to public offices, and that there should be full liberty of conscience. (4) That the Polish language should be used in the administration of law and education. (5) That there should be a regular and legal system of conscription.

Gortchakoff, in reply, maintained that the changes already conceded by the Emperor had gone some way in the direction of these six contentions of the British Government, and that it had been fully intended to carry them further, but that nothing could be done till the insurrection was put down. Lord Russell was not satisfied with these explanations and insisted upon his conditions. The correspondence ended by the Emperor giving his assurance that he was actuated by the most benevolent intentions towards Poland. "To provide for the welfare of his subjects of all races and of every religious conviction is an obligation which he has accepted before God, his conscience, and his people." *

As neither England nor France was prepared to support the Polish cause by war, nothing more came of this diplomatic remonstrance. Lord Palmerston in the House of Commons asserted that the British Government was entitled to take action on the breach of the Treaty of Vienna, but was under no positive obligation to do so. This view of the case was accepted by the House of Commons. There was no desire for active intervention.

Meanwhile the Russian army was engaged in putting down the insurgents. It was no easy task, as there was no central organized force opposed to them, which they could deal with and crush. There were sporadic outbreaks all over the country. The Prussians did their best to assist the Russians. Bismarck, who was then at the head of affairs in Prussia, entered into a convention with the Emperor, under which his Government agreed to assist in putting down the rebellion in Poland, by forming cordons of troops on the frontier to prevent the insurgents finding refuge in Prussian

* The correspondence is printed at length in the *Annual Register* for 1863.

Poland, and by authorizing the Russian troops to pursue them on Prussian territory, if they crossed the border. This co-operation in putting down the Polish revolt led to a good understanding with Russia, and enabled Bismarck to count with certainty on her friendly neutrality in his wars of 1866 and 1870 against Austria and France.

No quarter was given to the insurgents by the Russians, under General Berg. Those taken in arms were hanged. The Poles retorted by secret assassinations, and many obnoxious Russians were removed in this way. After many months the revolt came to an end, in May 1864. The régime of administrative severity was then renewed. The concessions made in 1861 were withdrawn. The expectations held out by Prince Gortchakoff, in his correspondence with Lord Russell in 1863, were not carried out. Every effort was again renewed to stamp out the Polish nationality, and to extinguish its language and religion. Roman Catholicism was vigorously attacked. The Church was deprived of its revenues. Three-fourths of the monasteries were suppressed. The village priests became the salaried officers of the State. The land belonging to the Church was put up for sale, and only Russians were allowed to bid for it.

A great scheme of agrarian reforms for Poland was then adopted by the Russian Government, in the hope of destroying its aristocratic classes, and of raising up the oppressed peasantry to be the pillars of support to Russia. It gave to the Polish cultivators the fee-simple of the land, which, since the abolition of serfdom, they had held as tenants at will. Indemnities, provided for loyal owners only, were charged on the revenues of Poland. A purposely undefined and uncertain right of access was given to the peasants to the forests and waste lands of the landowners.

In 1866, Poland was divided into four departments, which were put under the Minister of the Interior of Russia. In 1869 the Russian language only was prescribed for all official transactions. The use of the Polish language was forbidden in the churches and schools, in newspapers, over shop doors, and even in private conversation. In 1874 the vice-royalty was abolished, and in 1876 the Russian judicial system was introduced. Russification, therefore, was forced upon the country as far as the law and the administration could effect it. This policy, and the system which it involved, was maintained during the reign of Alexander III. The present Emperor, Nicholas II, has in recent years shown a desire to adopt a different and more conciliatory attitude to the Poles. The survivors of those who were deported to Siberia, after the outbreak of 1863, were allowed to return to their homes. A certain measure of freedom has been accorded to the Press. The Polish language is no longer forbidden in the churches and schools. The law forbidding landowners to sell their land to any but Russians has been repealed. There are other indications of an intention to make concessions.

Meanwhile the prosperity of Poland of late years, and till the outbreak of the present war, has been very marked. As a result of its unification with Russia, the custom-houses between the two countries were abolished, and complete freedom of trade was established between them. This has been of enormous advantage to the Poles. Their manufacturers have had the benefit of an open market to a country of 160 millions of people. Poland has large and most valuable coalfields. It has a great and rapidly growing population, well qualified for industrial manufactures. The high duties levied by the Russian Government on all imported manufactures have been specially to the advantage of Polish industries. Manufacturing towns, like Lodz, have sprung up with great rapidity. Factories have been established, often by Germans, or with German capital. Warsaw has quadrupled in population. The economic bearing of this on the political relation of Poland to Russia is evident. The complete independence of Poland, its severance from Russia, and the re-establishment of a cordon of customs-houses, with the Russian customs dues telling against the Polish manufacturers, instead of in their favour, would entail losses on a vast number of industries.

There is, further, the improvement in the condition of the peasantry, due to their emancipation from serfdom, and their being converted into owners of their holdings. Whether this has had the effect of reconciling the peasantry to Russian rule, in spite of the long efforts of the Government to stamp out their nationality, their religion, and their language, remains to be seen.

When we turn from Russia to Austria, the story of what has been effected since the

Treaty of Vienna is very different. For some years the rule of Austria in Galicia was very arbitrary and severe, and in no way conformable to the intentions of the Congress. In 1846, troubles of an agrarian character occurred in the district of Cracow, which had been created an independent republic, and the city became the centre of disturbance. The Austrian Government intervened, and forcibly annexed the little republic, without remonstrance, and probably with the approval of Russia and Prussia. In 1866, a fortunate change took place in the policy of Austria to the whole of Galicia. A very full measure of autonomy was conceded to it. A Diet was created, in which the use of Polish and Ruthenian languages was permitted. Religious toleration and equality and freedom of the Press were established. Attempts to interfere with the schools were abandoned. The province was given representation in the Imperial Reichstag by Polish and Ruthenian deputies. As a result the Poles of Galicia are now said to be loyal subjects of the Austrian Empire.

Galicia is at present the centre of intellectual life of the Polish race. It is the only country inhabited by them in which they are permitted to express themselves freely, in speech and writing, in their own language, where no attempt is made to prevent their free development, and where they can celebrate events connected with the past history of Poland. Poles form nearly 60 per cent. of the population of the province, and they have a much larger proportion of its wealth in their hands. The minority are Ruthenians. It has been alleged that, like many other majorities elsewhere, the Poles have, in the past, been disposed to treat the minority unfairly, to deny to them an adequate representation in the Diet, and to monopolize State appointments. However that may have been, an agreement has recently been arrived at between the leaders of the two races that representation in the Diet shall be divided between them in the proportion of three to two, and that State appointments shall be in the same ratio. On the whole, a more striking illustration of the value and success of Home Rule could not well be conceived than that in the Polish parts of Galicia.

The treatment by Prussia of the Polish provinces secured to it by the Congress of

Vienna has been the exact opposite to that of Austria. For some years, after the treaty of 1815, there was not much to complain of. The Poles in the Posen province, and elsewhere, were allowed a certain amount of local government, on the same lines as their German neighbours. The Polish peasants were admitted to the benefits of the Stein-Hardenberg land reforms, which freed them completely from serfdom, and gave them permanent interests in their holdings.

It was not till a few years after the consolidation of the German Empire, that Bismarck, alarmed by the relative increase of Poles to Germans in the provinces of West Prussia and Posen, adopted a new policy of pressure and severity against the former. In spite of the fact that the Polish conscripts had fought with the utmost bravery and loyalty for the Prussian cause, in his two great wars of 1866 and 1870 against Austria and France, he commenced a series of measures for Germanizing these provinces.

In 1885 he was responsible for an edict by which all Poles, who were not Prussian subjects, were expelled from Prussia. It appeared that a large number of Poles, natives of Russian Poland, had, of late years, established themselves in trades and professions in Prussia. Many of them had resided there a great number of years. They were now compelled, at the shortest notice, to give up their occupations and to leave the country with their families. The expulsion was carried out with great severity. No fewer than 34,700 persons were banished in this way, without the slightest compassion for them. No charge of conspiracy or disloyalty was preferred against them. Many of them had served in the Prussian army, and still belonged to the Landwehr. Many workmen who had for years been members of mutual relief societies in Prussia, and were entitled to provision in their old age, were now deprived of the results of their thrift. Many of them only spoke German, having resided so long in Prussia. It was difficult for them to find employment in Russian Poland. No distinctions were allowed. One and all were compelled to leave their homes.

This measure was defended on the ground that the interest of the State could not tolerate the presence in Prussia of large numbers of Poles who were not Prussian subjects, any more than it could allow Danes in Schleswig-Holstein or Frenchmen in Alsace and Lorraine. It was necessary to prevent the increase of Poles on Prussian territory. Bismarck refused to allow the subject to be discussed in the German Reichstag. When challenged on the subject, he read an Imperial message, declaring that the interpellation was based on the legal assumption of there being a Government in Germany, constitutionally capable of taking action to prevent the carrying out of measures which had been ordered by the Government in the Kingdom of Prussia, with regard to the expulsion of subjects of foreign States. Bismarck added that the measure had been taken in virtue of the Emperor's right, as King of Prussia, to protect the Germanic element in his border province against the flood of foreign nationalities, who were settling there to its detriment, and that it was entirely beyond the competency of the German Parliament to call on the King of Prussia to give an account of the way in which he exercised his sovereign rights in Prussia. He left the Chamber together with other members of his Government.

In 1886 Bismarck made his next effort to Germanize the Polish provinces of Prussia, by a scheme for colonizing the estates of Polish landowners with German peasants. He appointed a Land Commission, with power to purchase estates, and to divide them into small holdings. In his original proposal the Commission was to have power to expropriate the landowners, and to take their land compulsorily; but public opinion in Germany, at that time, would not stand this, and the measure, as passed, was restricted to the permissive power to purchase estates for the purpose. Very large transactions took place, and the Commission bought and cut up very numerous estates, and planted German peasant farmers upon them. The scheme, however, caused great indignation and excitement amongst the Poles of these districts. They were not slow in taking action to counteract this policy. The entry of the Commission into the land market caused the inflation of land values. The Polish landowners got very high prices for their land. Out of the proceeds many of them bought other properties from German owners, cut them up into small holdings, and settled Poles on them. Polish banks financed schemes for the purchase of German properties for the same purpose. It resulted that on the balance of the next twenty years, ending in 1906, there was an increase in the proportion of Poles to Germans in these districts, rather than the reverse, as was aimed at by the legislation of Bismarck. The economic and social coalitions of the two races also tended to promote this. The great increase of manufactures and industries in Westphalia and Silesia drew from the east of Prussia large numbers of its German workmen. They were replaced by workmen from Polish districts, where the increase of population was very great, and where the birth-rate has been higher than in any other part of Europe, while that of Germany, though still high compared to that of England, has been diminishing of late years. The result has been that even in the towns of East and West Prussia, where formerly the population was exclusively German, there has been a large influx of Poles, while in rural districts their predominance has been more than maintained, in spite of Bismarck's colonization scheme. Meanwhile, the Land Commission found increasing difficulty in acquiring properties, owing to the unwillingness of Polish landowners to sell.

In 1907 Prince von Bülow, on the part of the Prussian Government, made another exceptional effort to stem the tide of Polish population, and carried a measure through the Prussian Diet giving power to the Land Commission to expropriate Polish landowners by the compulsory purchase of their properties, at prices to be fixed by the authorities. Since his retirement Prince Bülow has published a defence of his policy in this respect, in a work recounting his achievements as Imperial Chancellor of Germany.

The Prince, following on the lines of Sybel and Carlyle, attributes the loss of its independence by Poland to the incapacity of its ruling class, and to the special intervention of Providence for its punishment, and for the aggrandizement of Germany.

"Although," he writes, "the Poles have forfeited their right to independence, after being for centuries incapable of creating a strong Government on the basis of law and order, yet none may shut their eyes to the tragic fate of this gifted and brave people." "The annexation of the Prussian States of our Eastern provinces, Posen and West Prussia, could not have come to pass if the Polish republic of nobles had been a State capable of continued existence. . . . What Providence has granted to us as a compensation for our losses elsewhere, our possessions in the East, these we must and will retain. . . . Because we prize our nationality so highly, we must respect the Poles and sympathize with the loyalty with which they cling to their national country." *

Having shed these and some other crocodile tears of sympathy for the poor Poles, he then

* Bülow's *Imperial Germany*. Translated by A. Lewenz, p. 257.

proceeds to justify his measures for expropriating their property and denationalizing them.

"No concern for the Polish people must hinder us from doing all we can to maintain and strengthen the German nationality in the former Polish provinces. Nobody dreams of wishing to thrust our Poles outside the borders of the Prussian kingdom. It is the duty, however, and the right of the Prussian Government to see that the Germans do not get driven out of the east of Germany by the Poles. The object is to protect, maintain, and strengthen the German nationality among the Poles. Consequently it is a fight for German nationality." *

"Under Bismarck," he says, "there began a determined fight for German nationality. Up till then the policy had been defensive, but under Bismarck Prussia began to take the offensive in order to rescue German nationality in the east, to maintain, and, if possible, to strengthen it.

"The Dispossession Bill makes the Commission independent of the variations of the estate marked, and ensures ultimate mastery to a strong Government in the economic struggle for the land."

"We ask that the Polish landowners shall be compelled in the national interest to place their land at the disposal of the State." †

We have quoted these passages at length, for they fully explain the recent policy of the Prussian Government towards its Polish subjects.

The law of 1907 met with great opposition on the part of the Poles. "We exist," said a

* Idem., p. 257. † Idem., p. 263.

Polish Deputy to the Diet, "in spite of exceptional laws, and those laws have nearly always been to the advantage of the Poles rather than of the Germans." Statistics are not yet to hand to show the result of the Dispossession Act of Prince Bülow, nor does he state in his defence what it has been. It is very certain, however, that in spite of an expenditure of many millions of pounds by the Prussian Government for the expropriation of Polish landowners since 1876, the balance of land in the hands of Poles in the Prussian Polish districts has increased by many thousands of acres, a striking proof of the failure of the policy.

Neither Bismarck nor Bülow was content with these measures for purchasing estates owned by Poles, and colonizing them with Germans. They also aimed at the extirpation of the Polish language. Up to 1872, Polish children were taught in their own language. A law was then passed forbidding this in future, and requiring that the children should only be taught in German. There still remained religious education, which was given in the native language of the children, but in 1888 it was enacted that if a majority of the children in a school were German, the minority should be taught to pray and say their creeds in German. Later this caused a strike among the children, instigated no doubt by their parents, and 100,000 children refused to receive religious teaching on these terms. Many of them were subjected to flogging on this account, and their parents were fined. In 1899 it was further directed that the schoolmasters, when Poles, were to cease the use of the Polish language in their family circles.

Prince Bülow, by way of defence for these measures, says:

> "We certainly do not wish to deprive the Poles of their native language, but we must try to bring it to pass that by means of the German language they will learn to understand the German spirit. We must proceed without severity, and this will increase or be mitigated as the Poles increase or diminish their opposition." *

The efforts of the Prussian Government to force the children of Poles to give up their native language have not been the only acts in this direction. At the present time no Pole is permitted to plead his own cause before the courts of law in his native language, and if he endeavours to employ it before the administrative authorities he will not be heard. Theatrical

* Bülow, p. 269.

performances in the Polish language are forbidden. Open-air meetings of Poles are not permitted. They can only take place in buildings under police supervision. The authorities also are able to insist on the Germanizing of Polish family names. Regulations of this kind and attempts to extirpate a language only cause exasperation. They have the opposite effect to what is intended and hoped for. They have caused more discontent and opposition even than the colonization scheme. The Polish peasants, who have undoubtedly gained material advantages since their annexation by Prussia, and who for long held aloof from any movements to regain their independence, have been driven into opposition, and have joined hands with the rest of their race.

These harsh measures of the Prussian Government explain how it is that Germany has never been able to win the confidence and loyalty of subject races. Whether it be the Poles in the east of Prussia, or the Danes in Schleswig-Holstein, or the French in Lorraine, they one and all regard German rule as oppressive and hateful, and long to be freed from it. Prussian statesmen have not learnt the secret, and have never tried the experiment, of treating alien races subject to them with sympathy, and according to them equality under the law and autonomy in local affairs.

How striking is the contrast between the results achieved by the Prussian methods and the conciliatory policy of Austria to the Poles of Galicia! Prince Bülow says that "Prussia could not possibly follow the Austrians' milder example in the treatment of the German Pole, for Prussia is the support of the German Empire, and of the national idea, and could not grant concessions, without being false to her past, her traditions, and her German mission."

Of the Prussian methods, it must be repeated that they are in direct conflict with the provisions of the Treaty of Vienna, and with the promises of Frederick William III, on taking possession of the province of Posen in 1815. But it is a matter of course with Prussian statesmen, from the times of Frederick the Great and Bismarck to the present, that neither treaty obligations nor kingly promises are of any value whatever, when Ministers of the day think that the interest of the State is opposed to them.

It will be seen from the above description of the treatment of the Poles by the three great Powers who were concerned in the dismemberment of their State, how great are the differences. Austria has been the only one of the three which has succeeded in winning the loyalty of the Poles subjected to it, by conceding to them a full autonomy. Germany, or rather Prussia, for the legislation and administration affecting the Poles has not been by the Imperial Reichstag, but by the Prussian Diet, has been the least successful of the three, and its Government is the most hated by the Poles. All three, however, within the last few months, since the outbreak of war, have stood before Europe in white sheets, and have confessed their errors in the partitions of Poland in 1772 and 1793-5. All three have made bold bids for the support of the Poles, and have, by public manifestoes, announced that, if successful, they will do their best to reunite the severed provinces of Poland, and to accord to them full autonomy, religious equality, and the use of the Polish language.

It is one of the main issues of the war whether these promises are to be fulfilled by Russia alone, or by Austria and Prussia combined. It is not possible for us in England to envisage any other result of the war than the success of our Allies. In such case, the task of reconstituting Poland will fall to Russia, subject, it must be presumed, to another Congress of the Powers of Europe. In any case, however, it would seem to be premature at present to discuss the details of a scheme for the reconstitution of Poland. A review of the past history of partitions and repartitions, and of promises of autonomy made and broken, and a study of the map of ethnological Poland, and of its neighbouring races, will show that many questions must arise most difficult of solution.

How, for instance, are the boundaries of a reunited Poland to be drawn? Are they to include the whole of West Prussia so as to give access to the sea? In such case, will East Prussia be again separated from Brandenburg and Germany as it was in olden time, or will it be included in the reconstituted Poland?

It may be well at this point to quote the opinion of Bismarck in a conversation recorded in the Memoirs of the eminent Italian statesman Crispi on September 17, 1877:

"The resurrection of Poland could not come about without the loss of a part of our territory. We should have to relinquish Thorn and Danzig. The German Empire would remain exposed on the Russian frontier, and we should lose our outlet on the Baltic."

Again, in his Memoirs Bismarck wrote:

> "In the Polish question Austria is confronted by no such difficulties as for us are indissolubly bound up with the re-establishment of Polish independence—difficulties incident to the adjustment of the respective claims of Poles and Germans in Poland and West Prussia and to the situation of East Prussia. Our geographical position and the intermixture of both nationalities in the eastern province, including Silesia, compel us to retard, as far as possible, the opening of the Polish question."

And again later he wrote:

> "Any arrangement likely to satisfy Poland in the provinces of West Prussia and Posen, and even in Silesia, is impossible without the breaking up and decomposing of Prussia." *

It must be admitted that, from a purely German point of view, there is much force in these contentions of Bismarck. We can well believe that Imperial Germany will not submit to the humiliation of surrendering her province of West Prussia to a reconstituted Poland, until driven to the last extremity by overwhelming defeat. There is, however, another side to the question from the point of view of Poland. Is it reasonable and right that twenty millions of Poles should be permanently

* *Reflections of Prince Bismarck.* English translation, i. 242.

deprived of organic constitution as a State, whether independent or under the supremacy of Russia, because of the opposing interest of Germany in three-fourths of a million of Prussians in West Prussia, or that a reconstituted Poland should be cut off from access to the sea because half a million of these people inhabit a belt of territory separating mainly Polish districts from the Baltic? Better, the Poles may say, that these comparatively few Prussians should be incorporated with Poland, than that three millions of Poles should continue to suffer from Prussian oppression! It must be admitted that it will be difficult to find a solution of this question based on the principle only of nationality. It will be well to recollect that the scheme which Russia is now contending for, on behalf of Poland, and which, it must be assumed, her Allies are supporting by their armed forces, is nearly identical, so far as territorial arrangements are concerned, with that which the Emperor Alexander proposed at the Congress of Vienna, and which Great Britain, in concert with Austria and Prussia, succeeded in defeating. It was not the only occasion, to use the metaphor of the late Lord Salisbury, on which this country put its money on the wrong horse.

The solution of these and many other questions will depend on the balance of forces which will exist, when the war is brought to a close. Whatever may be the decision on such points, we may confidently hope that Europe will not repeat the mistake, which it made a hundred years ago, at the Congress of Vienna, and that a reconstituted Poland will take its place again, if not with complete independence, at least as an assured nationality which, by unity and strength, will be able in the future to assert and defend its liberties.

INDEX

21